Get A Free Book At: xspurts.com/posts/free-book-offer

Table of Contents:

Exit Strategy and Selling Your Business

Have Questions / Comments?

Get Another Book Free

Starting Your Own Mobile Car Washing Service

Starting your own mobile car washing service can be an exciting venture for entrepreneurs looking to break into the automotive service industry. With the convenience and efficiency of providing car cleaning services directly to customers at their homes or workplaces, mobile car washing has become increasingly popular. However, launching a successful mobile car washing business requires careful planning, dedication, and attention to detail.

One of the first steps in starting a mobile car washing service is to create a comprehensive business plan. This plan should outline your target market, pricing strategy, marketing tactics, and operational procedures. Conducting market research to identify potential customers and competitors in your area is crucial for developing a competitive edge.

Investing in high-quality equipment and cleaning products is essential for delivering top-notch service to your customers. Portable pressure washers, water tanks, eco-friendly detergents, and detailing tools are some of the basic supplies you'll need to get started. Additionally, consider investing in a reliable vehicle to transport your equipment and reach customers efficiently.

Building a strong online presence is vital for attracting customers to your mobile car washing service. Create a professional website showcasing your services, pricing, and contact information. Utilize social media platforms to engage with potential customers, share before-and-after photos of your work, and offer special promotions to incentivize bookings.

Networking with local businesses and community organizations can also help generate leads for your mobile car washing service. Partnering with auto dealerships, corporate offices, residential complexes, and event organizers can provide a steady stream of clients and recurring contracts.

Providing exceptional customer service is key to retaining clients and building a positive reputation for your mobile car washing business. Be punctual, courteous, and attentive to your customers' needs and preferences. Offer flexible scheduling options and customizable service packages to accommodate diverse clientele.

Implementing eco-friendly practices in your mobile car washing operations can set you apart from competitors and appeal to environmentally conscious customers. Consider using biodegradable cleaning products, conserving water, and recycling wastewater responsibly. Communicate your commitment to sustainability to attract eco-minded clientele and contribute to a greener future.

As your mobile car washing business grows, consider expanding your service offerings to meet evolving customer demands. In addition to exterior washing and detailing, consider offering interior cleaning, waxing, polishing, and odor removal services. Providing a comprehensive range of services can increase your revenue potential and enhance customer satisfaction.

Maintaining proper insurance coverage is essential for protecting your mobile car washing business against unforeseen risks and liabilities. Consult with an insurance agent to determine the appropriate coverage options for your specific needs, including liability insurance, commercial auto insurance, and property insurance.

Regularly evaluating and refining your business strategies is essential for long-term success in the competitive mobile car washing industry. Stay informed about industry trends, customer preferences, and technological advancements to stay ahead of the curve. Solicit feedback from customers to identify areas for improvement and implement changes accordingly.

In conclusion, starting your own mobile car washing service can be a rewarding and lucrative endeavor for aspiring entrepreneurs. By following these tips and strategies, you can launch and grow a successful mobile car washing business that delights customers and stands out in the market.

Understanding the Mobile Car Wash Industry

The Mobile Car Wash Industry: A Comprehensive Guide

The mobile car wash industry has experienced significant growth in recent years, driven by changing consumer preferences, technological advancements, and environmental awareness. Understanding the dynamics of this industry is essential for entrepreneurs looking to capitalize on its potential and navigate its challenges effectively.

Mobile car washing services offer convenience and flexibility to customers by bringing car cleaning directly to their homes, workplaces, or wherever they may be. This on-demand approach has gained popularity due to its time-saving benefits and the ability to maintain vehicles without the hassle of traditional car washes.

One of the key factors driving the growth of the mobile car wash industry is the increasing emphasis on sustainability and eco-friendliness. Many mobile car wash operators utilize water-saving techniques, biodegradable cleaning products, and eco-friendly practices to minimize their environmental impact. This aligns with the preferences of environmentally conscious consumers who prioritize businesses that prioritize sustainability.

Technological advancements have also played a significant role in shaping the mobile car wash industry. Mobile apps and online platforms have made it easier for customers to book and schedule car wash services with just a few taps on their smartphones. These platforms often offer features such as real-time tracking of service providers, secure payment options, and customer reviews, enhancing the overall experience for both customers and service providers.

Moreover, the availability of high-quality cleaning equipment and products has enabled mobile car wash operators to deliver professional-level results without the need for a fixed location. Portable pressure washers, steam cleaners, and advanced detailing tools allow for thorough cleaning and detailing of vehicles, regardless of their location.

The mobile car wash industry also offers opportunities for entrepreneurs to enter the market with relatively low startup costs compared to traditional car wash businesses. With minimal overhead expenses such as rent and utilities, mobile car wash operators can focus their resources on acquiring equipment, marketing their services, and expanding their customer base.

However, despite its many advantages, the mobile car wash industry also faces challenges that operators must navigate to succeed. One of the main challenges is maintaining a consistent customer base in the face of competition from traditional car wash businesses and other mobile operators. Building brand loyalty through exceptional service, competitive pricing, and effective marketing is essential for retaining customers and sustaining long-term growth.

Additionally, mobile car wash operators must ensure compliance with local regulations and environmental guidelines governing water usage, wastewater disposal, and chemical handling. Failure to adhere to these regulations can result in fines, penalties, and damage to the reputation of the business.

Furthermore, the seasonal nature of the car wash industry can pose challenges for mobile operators, with demand fluctuating depending on factors such as weather conditions and economic trends. Diversifying services, targeting new customer segments, and offering promotions during slower periods can help mitigate the impact of seasonality on business operations.

In conclusion, the mobile car wash industry offers lucrative opportunities for entrepreneurs seeking to enter the automotive service sector. By understanding the key drivers, trends, and challenges shaping the industry, aspiring mobile car wash operators can position themselves for success and capitalize on the growing demand for convenient and sustainable car cleaning solutions.

Market Research

Market Research: The Key to Success in the Mobile Car Washing Industry

Market research plays a crucial role in the success of any business, including mobile car washing services. Understanding the market landscape, customer preferences, and competitive dynamics is essential for identifying opportunities, making informed decisions, and developing effective strategies to grow and thrive in the industry.

One of the primary objectives of market research for mobile car washing services is to identify the target market and understand its needs and preferences. This involves gathering demographic information such as age, income level, location, and vehicle ownership patterns to pinpoint the most lucrative customer segments. By understanding who their potential customers are, mobile car wash operators can tailor their services and marketing efforts to better meet their needs and attract their business.

Furthermore, conducting market research helps mobile car wash operators assess the demand for their services in specific geographic areas. Analyzing factors such as population density, traffic patterns, and local economic conditions can provide valuable insights into the potential size of the market and the level of competition. Identifying underserved or overlooked areas can present opportunities for mobile car wash operators to establish a foothold and capture market share.

Another critical aspect of market research for mobile car washing services is analyzing customer preferences and behavior. This involves gathering feedback through surveys, interviews, and online reviews to understand what customers value most in a car washing service. Factors such as convenience, affordability, quality of service, and environmental sustainability are often cited as important considerations for consumers when choosing a car wash provider. By listening to customer feedback and adjusting their offerings accordingly, mobile car wash operators can enhance customer satisfaction and loyalty.

Moreover, market research helps mobile car wash operators stay abreast of industry trends and emerging technologies that could impact their business. Keeping tabs on developments such as new cleaning techniques, eco-friendly products, and mobile app innovations allows operators to adapt and innovate to stay competitive in the rapidly evolving market landscape. Additionally, monitoring competitor activities and pricing strategies can provide valuable insights into market dynamics and help inform strategic decision-making.

In addition to understanding the demand side of the market, market research also involves assessing the supply side, including competitors and potential collaborators. Analyzing the strengths and weaknesses of existing car wash businesses in the area can help mobile operators identify gaps in the market and develop a unique value proposition. Furthermore, establishing partnerships with complementary businesses such as auto dealerships, corporate offices, and residential complexes can provide access to a steady stream of customers and help expand the reach of mobile car washing services.

In conclusion, market research is a critical tool for mobile car wash operators seeking to succeed in the competitive automotive service industry. By gathering and analyzing data on market demand, customer preferences, industry trends, and competitor activities, operators can gain valuable insights to inform their decision-making and develop strategies for growth and differentiation. Investing time and resources in comprehensive market research can pay dividends in the form of increased customer satisfaction, business growth, and long-term success.

Business Plan Development

Crafting a Solid Business Plan for Your Mobile Car Washing Venture

Launching a mobile car washing service can be an exciting endeavor, but it requires careful planning and preparation to ensure success. One of the most crucial steps in starting any business, including a mobile car washing service, is developing a comprehensive business plan. A well-thought-out business plan serves as a roadmap for your venture, outlining your goals, strategies, and tactics for achieving success.

The first step in developing a business plan for your mobile car washing service is defining your vision and mission. What do you hope to achieve with your business, and what values will guide your operations? Clearly articulating your vision and mission will help you stay focused and aligned as you navigate the challenges and opportunities that arise.

Next, conduct thorough market research to understand the demand for mobile car washing services in your target area. Analyze factors such as population demographics, vehicle ownership rates, and competitor landscape to identify potential opportunities and challenges. Understanding your market will inform your pricing strategy, marketing efforts, and service offerings.

Once you have a clear understanding of your market and target audience, it's time to develop a marketing plan. Identify the most effective channels for reaching your target customers, whether it's through digital advertising, social media marketing, local partnerships, or word-of-mouth referrals. Determine your unique selling proposition and craft compelling messaging that highlights the benefits of your mobile car washing service.

In addition to marketing, your business plan should also outline your operational plan, including your service offerings, equipment needs, and staffing requirements. Determine what services you will offer, such as exterior washing, interior detailing, waxing, or additional add-ons. Invest in high-quality equipment and supplies to deliver professional-level results, and consider hiring experienced staff or partnering with independent contractors to help meet customer demand.

Financial planning is another critical component of your business plan. Estimate your startup costs, including equipment purchases, vehicle expenses, insurance, marketing expenses, and any other initial investments. Develop a detailed budget and revenue projections to ensure that your business is financially viable and sustainable in the long term. Consider factors such as pricing strategy, customer volume, and seasonal fluctuations in demand when projecting your revenue and expenses.

Finally, your business plan should include a risk management strategy to identify and mitigate potential risks to your business. This could include risks such as equipment breakdowns, liability issues, or changes in market conditions. Develop contingency plans to address these risks and ensure that your business can adapt and thrive in any situation.

In conclusion, developing a solid business plan is essential for launching a successful mobile car washing service. By defining your vision and mission, conducting thorough market research, developing a marketing plan, outlining your operational strategy, and creating a financial plan, you can set your business up for success and position yourself for long-term growth and profitability. With a clear roadmap in place, you'll be well-equipped to navigate the challenges and opportunities of the mobile car washing industry and build a thriving business that delights customers and drives results.

Legal Framework for Mobile Car Wash Businesses

Navigating the Legal Landscape: Ensuring Compliance for Your Mobile Car Washing Business

Operating a mobile car washing business can be an exciting venture, offering convenience and flexibility to both operators and customers alike. However, like any business, mobile car wash operators must adhere to a variety of legal requirements and regulations to ensure compliance and mitigate potential risks. Understanding the legal framework governing mobile car washing businesses is essential for maintaining a successful and sustainable operation.

One of the primary legal considerations for mobile car wash businesses is obtaining the necessary licenses and permits to operate legally. The specific requirements vary depending on location, but commonly include business licenses, permits for water usage and discharge, environmental permits, and any other relevant permits mandated by local authorities. Failure to obtain the required licenses and permits can result in fines, penalties, or even the shutdown of your business, so it's essential to research and comply with all applicable regulations.

Environmental regulations are another important aspect of the legal framework for mobile car wash businesses. Because mobile car washing involves the use of water and cleaning chemicals, operators must ensure that their activities comply with environmental laws aimed at protecting water quality and minimizing pollution. This may include using eco-friendly cleaning products, implementing water-saving techniques, and properly disposing of wastewater according to local regulations. By adopting environmentally sustainable practices, mobile car wash operators can not only comply with legal requirements but also appeal to environmentally conscious customers and enhance their reputation.

Insurance is another critical consideration for mobile car wash businesses. Accidents can happen, whether it's damage to a customer's vehicle, injuries to employees, or other unforeseen incidents. Having adequate insurance coverage can protect your business from potential liabilities and financial losses. Common types of insurance for mobile car wash businesses include general liability insurance, commercial auto insurance, workers' compensation insurance, and equipment insurance. Consult with an insurance professional to determine the appropriate coverage for your specific needs and ensure that your business is adequately protected.

Additionally, mobile car wash operators must comply with employment laws and regulations when hiring and managing employees. This includes adhering to minimum wage laws, providing a safe working environment, and complying with regulations related to employee benefits and taxes. Depending on the size and structure of your business, you may also need to comply with additional labor laws such as overtime pay, family and medical leave, and anti-discrimination laws. Staying informed about employment laws and seeking legal advice when necessary can help ensure that your business operates ethically and legally.

Intellectual property considerations are also important for mobile car wash businesses, particularly when it comes to branding and marketing. Protecting your business name, logo, and other intellectual property assets through trademarks and copyrights can prevent others from using them without your permission and help build brand recognition and loyalty. Conducting a trademark search and consulting with a legal professional can help ensure that your intellectual property rights are protected.

In conclusion, understanding and complying with the legal framework governing mobile car wash businesses is essential for success in the industry. By obtaining the necessary licenses and permits, adhering to environmental regulations, securing adequate insurance coverage, complying with employment laws, and protecting intellectual property rights, mobile car wash operators can operate legally, ethically, and responsibly while minimizing risks and liabilities. By prioritizing compliance and legal integrity, mobile car wash businesses can build a strong foundation for long-term success and sustainability.

Registering the Business

Navigating the Process: Registering Your Mobile Car Washing Business

Registering your mobile car washing business is a crucial step in establishing a legitimate and compliant operation. Whether you're a sole proprietor or planning to form a partnership or corporation, understanding the registration process is essential for ensuring legal compliance and protecting your business interests.

The first step in registering your mobile car washing business is choosing a business structure that best suits your needs. Common options include sole proprietorship, partnership, limited liability company (LLC), or corporation. Each structure has its own advantages and disadvantages in terms of liability, taxation, and management flexibility. Consider consulting with a legal or financial advisor to determine the most appropriate structure for your business.

Once you've decided on a business structure, you'll need to register your business name with the appropriate government authorities. This typically involves conducting a business name search to ensure that your chosen name is available and not already in use by another business. Depending on your location, you may need to register your business name with the state, county, or city government. Additionally, if you plan to operate under a name other than your own, you may need to file a "Doing Business As" (DBA) or fictitious name registration.

After registering your business name, you'll need to obtain any required business licenses and permits to operate legally. The specific licenses and permits needed vary depending on your location and the nature of your business, but common requirements for mobile car washing businesses include a general business license, water usage permit, environmental permit, and possibly others. Research the licensing requirements in your area and ensure that you obtain all necessary permits before launching your business.

In addition to obtaining business licenses and permits, you may also need to register your business for taxation purposes. This typically involves obtaining an Employer Identification Number (EIN) from the Internal Revenue Service (IRS), which is used to identify your business for tax reporting purposes. Even if you don't have employees, obtaining an EIN is often necessary for opening a business bank account, filing taxes, and other administrative purposes.

If you plan to hire employees for your mobile car washing business, you'll need to register with state and federal employment agencies for tax and reporting purposes. This may involve registering with your state's labor department for state unemployment insurance and workers' compensation coverage, as well as obtaining an employer identification number (EIN) from the IRS for federal tax withholding and reporting.

Finally, don't forget to register your business with any relevant industry associations or organizations. Joining industry associations can provide valuable networking opportunities, access to resources and training, and credibility for your business. Additionally, consider obtaining business insurance to protect your assets and mitigate risks associated with operating a mobile car washing business.

In conclusion, registering your mobile car washing business is a critical step in establishing a legitimate and compliant operation. By choosing the right business structure, registering your business name, obtaining necessary licenses and permits, registering for taxation purposes, and joining industry associations, you can ensure that your business is legally compliant and positioned for success. Take the time to research and understand the registration process in your area, and seek professional guidance when necessary to ensure that you meet all legal requirements and set your business up for long-term growth and success.

Insurance and Permit Needs

Protecting Your Business: Understanding Insurance and Permit Needs for Mobile Car Washing Services

Operating a mobile car washing service comes with its own set of risks and liabilities, which is why having the right insurance coverage and permits in place is essential for protecting your business and ensuring compliance with regulations. From liability insurance to environmental permits, understanding your insurance and permit needs is crucial for maintaining a successful and sustainable operation.

One of the most important types of insurance for mobile car washing businesses is general liability insurance. This coverage protects your business against claims of bodily injury or property damage that may occur during the course of your operations. For example, if a customer slips and falls while their car is being washed, general liability insurance would cover the cost of medical expenses or property damage resulting from the incident. Without this coverage, your business could be held financially responsible for such claims, leading to costly legal fees and potential settlements.

In addition to general liability insurance, mobile car washing businesses may also need commercial auto insurance to protect their vehicles and equipment. Commercial auto insurance provides coverage for accidents, theft, vandalism, and other damages to your vehicles while they are being used for business purposes. This coverage is essential for protecting your investment in your mobile car washing equipment and ensuring that you can continue operating in the event of an accident or other unforeseen circumstances.

Workers' compensation insurance is another important consideration for mobile car washing businesses that have employees. This coverage provides benefits to employees who are injured or become ill as a result of their work. Workers' compensation insurance typically covers medical expenses, lost wages, and rehabilitation costs for injured employees, helping to protect both your employees and your business from the financial impact of workplace injuries.

In addition to insurance coverage, mobile car washing businesses may also need to obtain various permits and licenses to operate legally. These permits may include environmental permits for water usage and wastewater discharge, business licenses from local authorities, and any other permits required by state or federal regulations. Failure to obtain the necessary permits could result in fines, penalties, or even the shutdown of your business, so it's essential to research and comply with all applicable regulations.

Environmental permits are particularly important for mobile car washing businesses, as they often involve the use of water and cleaning chemicals that can impact the environment if not managed properly. Depending on your location, you may need permits for water usage, wastewater discharge, and chemical handling. Additionally, implementing environmentally sustainable practices such as using eco-friendly cleaning products and water-saving techniques can help reduce your environmental impact and demonstrate your commitment to responsible business practices.

In conclusion, insurance coverage and permits are essential for protecting your mobile car washing business and ensuring compliance with regulations. General liability insurance, commercial auto insurance, and workers' compensation insurance can help protect your business against financial losses resulting from accidents, injuries, or property damage. Additionally, obtaining the necessary permits and licenses, including environmental permits, business licenses, and any other permits required by local authorities, is essential for operating legally and responsibly. By understanding your insurance and permit needs and taking the necessary steps to protect your business, you can minimize risks, safeguard your assets, and build a successful and sustainable mobile car washing operation.

Regulatory Compliance

Staying on the Right Side of the Law: Navigating Regulatory Compliance for Mobile Car Washing Services

Operating a mobile car washing service offers flexibility and convenience, but it also comes with a host of regulatory requirements that must be met to ensure compliance and avoid potential legal issues. From environmental regulations to employment laws, understanding and adhering to regulatory requirements is essential for maintaining a successful and sustainable business.

One of the primary areas of regulatory compliance for mobile car washing services is environmental regulations. Because mobile car washing involves the use of water and cleaning chemicals, operators must take precautions to minimize their environmental impact and comply with laws aimed at protecting water quality and preventing pollution. This may include obtaining permits for water usage and wastewater discharge, implementing water-saving techniques, and using eco-friendly cleaning products. By adhering to environmental regulations, mobile car washing operators can demonstrate their commitment to sustainability and responsible business practices.

In addition to environmental regulations, mobile car washing businesses must also comply with various employment laws and regulations. This includes adhering to minimum wage laws, providing a safe working environment, and complying with regulations related to employee benefits and taxes. Depending on the size and structure of the business, operators may also need to comply with additional labor laws such as overtime pay, family and medical leave, and anti-discrimination laws. Staying informed about employment laws and seeking legal advice when necessary can help ensure that mobile car washing businesses operate ethically and legally.

Furthermore, mobile car washing operators must obtain the necessary licenses and permits to operate legally. This may include business licenses from local authorities, environmental permits for water usage and discharge, and any other permits required by state or federal regulations. Failure to obtain the required licenses and permits can result in fines, penalties, or even the shutdown of the business, so it's essential to research and comply with all applicable regulations.

Insurance coverage is another critical aspect of regulatory compliance for mobile car washing businesses. General liability insurance, commercial auto insurance, and workers' compensation insurance can help protect the business against financial losses resulting from accidents, injuries, or property damage. Additionally, obtaining adequate insurance coverage demonstrates to customers and stakeholders that the business is committed to operating responsibly and ethically.

Moreover, mobile car washing operators must comply with advertising regulations and consumer protection laws. This includes ensuring that advertising materials are truthful and not misleading, disclosing any material terms and conditions to customers, and protecting consumer privacy and data. By following advertising regulations and consumer protection laws, mobile car washing businesses can build trust and credibility with their customers and avoid potential legal disputes.

In conclusion, regulatory compliance is a critical aspect of operating a mobile car washing service. By understanding and adhering to environmental regulations, employment laws, licensing requirements, insurance coverage, and advertising regulations, mobile car washing operators can ensure that their businesses operate legally and responsibly. Staying informed about regulatory requirements and seeking legal advice when necessary can help minimize risks and liabilities and build a successful and sustainable mobile car washing business.

Financing a Mobile Car Wash

Securing Funds: Financing Options for Your Mobile Car Washing Venture

Launching a mobile car washing service requires careful planning and financial investment. From purchasing equipment to marketing your business, securing the necessary funds is essential for turning your entrepreneurial vision into reality. Fortunately, there are various financing options available to help you finance your mobile car wash and get your business off the ground.

One common financing option for mobile car washing businesses is bootstrapping, or using personal savings and resources to fund the startup costs. This approach allows entrepreneurs to retain full control of their business and avoid taking on debt or giving up equity. While bootstrapping may require significant personal investment, it can be a viable option for those who have the financial means to self-finance their business.

Another financing option for mobile car washing businesses is obtaining a traditional bank loan or line of credit. Banks and financial institutions offer a variety of loan products designed specifically for small businesses, including term loans, SBA loans, and lines of credit. These loans typically require a strong credit history, a solid business plan, and collateral to secure the loan. While traditional bank loans may offer competitive interest rates and favorable repayment terms, they can be difficult to qualify for, especially for new businesses without a proven track record.

Alternatively, mobile car washing operators may explore alternative lending options such as online lenders, peer-to-peer lending platforms, or crowdfunding campaigns. These alternative financing sources often have less stringent qualification criteria than traditional banks and may offer faster approval and funding processes. However, alternative lenders may charge higher interest rates or fees, so it's essential to carefully evaluate the terms and conditions before committing to a loan.

In addition to loans, mobile car washing operators may consider seeking investment from outside investors or venture capitalists. Angel investors, venture capital firms, and private equity investors may be willing to provide funding in exchange for equity in the business. While this option can provide access to significant capital and expertise, it also involves giving up a portion of ownership and control of the business. Mobile car washing operators should carefully consider the implications of accepting outside investment and ensure that the terms of any investment agreement align with their long-term goals and vision for the business.

Furthermore, mobile car washing operators may explore government grants and incentives available to small businesses in their area. Many governments offer grants, loans, or tax incentives to encourage entrepreneurship and small business growth. These programs may be targeted at specific industries, regions, or demographics and may require applicants to meet certain eligibility criteria. Researching government funding programs and consulting with local business development agencies can help mobile car washing operators identify potential funding opportunities.

Lastly, mobile car washing operators may consider partnering with equipment suppliers or franchisors who offer financing or leasing options for their equipment. Equipment financing or leasing allows businesses to acquire the necessary equipment without requiring a large upfront investment. Instead, businesses make regular payments over time, making it easier to manage cash flow and preserve capital for other business expenses. Additionally, equipment financing may offer tax benefits such as depreciation deductions or lease payments that may be deductible as business expenses.

In conclusion, financing a mobile car washing business requires careful consideration of the available options and their implications for the long-term success of the business. Whether through personal savings, traditional bank loans, alternative lending sources, investment from outside investors, government grants, or equipment financing, mobile car washing operators have a variety of financing options available to them. By carefully evaluating their financing needs and exploring all available options, entrepreneurs can secure the necessary funds to launch and grow a successful mobile car washing venture.

Start-up Costs

Counting the Costs: Understanding Start-up Expenses for Mobile Car Washing Services

Launching a mobile car washing service can be an exciting entrepreneurial venture, but it requires careful planning and consideration of start-up costs. From equipment and supplies to marketing and insurance, understanding the expenses involved is essential for budgeting and securing the necessary funds to get your business off the ground.

One of the primary start-up costs for a mobile car washing service is equipment. High-quality cleaning equipment, including pressure washers, steam cleaners, vacuums, and detailing tools, is essential for delivering professional-level results. Additionally, you'll need water tanks, hoses, and storage containers to transport water and cleaning products to your customers' locations. Investing in reliable equipment is crucial for providing efficient and effective service to your clients.

In addition to equipment, mobile car washing operators must budget for supplies such as cleaning products, towels, brushes, and protective gear. Eco-friendly cleaning products are often preferred by environmentally conscious customers and may come at a higher cost than traditional chemical-based products. However, investing in eco-friendly supplies can help attract environmentally conscious clientele and differentiate your business from competitors.

Furthermore, mobile car washing operators must consider vehicle expenses when budgeting for start-up costs. Whether purchasing or leasing a vehicle, such as a van or truck, to transport equipment and reach customers, there are associated costs such as vehicle purchase or lease payments, insurance, fuel, maintenance, and repairs. Choosing a reliable and fuel-efficient vehicle that can accommodate your equipment and branding is essential for operating a successful mobile car washing business.

Marketing and advertising expenses are another important consideration for mobile car washing start-ups. Building brand awareness and attracting customers requires investment in marketing materials such as business cards, flyers, signage, and branded apparel. Additionally, digital marketing channels such as website development, search engine optimization (SEO), social media advertising, and online listings can help reach potential customers and generate leads. Allocating a portion of your budget to marketing and advertising efforts is essential for growing your customer base and establishing a strong presence in the market.

Insurance coverage is also a significant start-up cost for mobile car washing businesses. General liability insurance, commercial auto insurance, workers' compensation insurance, and equipment insurance are all essential for protecting your business against potential risks and liabilities. While insurance premiums may vary depending on factors such as coverage limits, deductibles, and the size of your operation, investing in adequate insurance coverage is essential for safeguarding your assets and mitigating financial risks.

Moreover, mobile car washing operators must budget for administrative expenses such as business licenses, permits, legal fees, and accounting services. Depending on your location and the nature of your business, you may need to obtain various permits and licenses to operate legally. Consulting with legal and financial professionals can help ensure that you comply with all regulatory requirements and avoid potential legal issues down the line.

Finally, it's essential to budget for contingencies and unforeseen expenses when planning for start-up costs. Unexpected challenges or emergencies may arise during the early stages of your business, so having a financial cushion in place can help cover unexpected expenses and ensure that your business remains resilient and adaptable.

In conclusion, understanding and budgeting for start-up costs is essential for launching a successful mobile car washing service. From equipment and supplies to marketing and insurance, there are various expenses involved in starting and operating a mobile car washing business. By carefully planning and budgeting for these costs, entrepreneurs can set themselves up for success and position their businesses for long-term growth and profitability.

Funding Options

Exploring Your Options: Funding Your Mobile Car Washing Business

Securing funding is a crucial step in launching and growing a mobile car washing business. Whether you're just starting out or looking to expand your operations, there are various funding options available to help you finance your business venture and achieve your goals.

One of the most common funding options for mobile car washing businesses is bootstrapping, or using personal savings and resources to fund the startup costs. Bootstrapping allows entrepreneurs to maintain full control of their business and avoid taking on debt or giving up equity. While bootstrapping may require significant personal investment, it can be a viable option for those who have the financial means to self-finance their business.

Another financing option for mobile car washing businesses is obtaining a traditional bank loan or line of credit. Banks and financial institutions offer a variety of loan products designed specifically for small businesses, including term loans, SBA loans, and lines of credit. These loans typically require a strong credit history, a solid business plan, and collateral to secure the loan. While traditional bank loans may offer competitive interest rates and favorable repayment terms, they can be difficult to qualify for, especially for new businesses without a proven track record.

Alternatively, mobile car washing operators may explore alternative lending options such as online lenders, peer-to-peer lending platforms, or crowdfunding campaigns. These alternative financing sources often have less stringent qualification criteria than traditional banks and may offer faster approval and funding processes. However, alternative lenders may charge higher interest rates or fees, so it's essential to carefully evaluate the terms and conditions before committing to a loan.

In addition to loans, mobile car washing operators may consider seeking investment from outside investors or venture capitalists. Angel investors, venture capital firms, and private equity investors may be willing to provide funding in exchange for equity in the business. While this option can provide access to significant capital and expertise, it also involves giving up a portion of ownership and control of the business. Mobile car washing operators should carefully consider the implications of accepting outside investment and ensure that the terms of any investment agreement align with their long-term goals and vision for the business.

Furthermore, mobile car washing operators may explore government grants and incentives available to small businesses in their area. Many governments offer grants, loans, or tax incentives to encourage entrepreneurship and small business growth. These programs may be targeted at specific industries, regions, or demographics and may require applicants to meet certain eligibility criteria. Researching government funding programs and consulting with local business development agencies can help mobile car washing operators identify potential funding opportunities.

Lastly, mobile car washing operators may consider partnering with equipment suppliers or franchisors who offer financing or leasing options for their equipment. Equipment financing or leasing allows businesses to acquire the necessary equipment without requiring a large upfront investment. Instead, businesses make regular payments over time, making it easier to manage cash flow and preserve capital for other business expenses. Additionally, equipment financing may offer tax benefits such as depreciation deductions or lease payments that may be deductible as business expenses.

In conclusion, funding your mobile car washing business requires careful consideration of the available options and their implications for the long-term success of the business. Whether through personal savings, traditional bank loans, alternative lending sources, investment from outside investors, government grants, or equipment financing, mobile car washing operators have a variety of funding options available to them. By carefully evaluating their funding needs and exploring all available options, entrepreneurs can secure the necessary funds to launch and grow a successful mobile car washing venture.

Money Management Strategies

Effective Money Management for Your Mobile Car Washing Business

Managing finances is a critical aspect of running any business, including a mobile car washing service. Implementing effective money management strategies can help mobile car washing operators optimize cash flow, minimize expenses, and maximize profitability. From budgeting and tracking expenses to managing accounts receivable and investing in growth, here are some key money management strategies for mobile car washing businesses.

One of the first steps in effective money management is creating a detailed budget that outlines your projected income and expenses. This budget should include all costs associated with running your mobile car washing business, including equipment purchases or leases, supplies, vehicle expenses, marketing and advertising, insurance premiums, permits and licenses, and any other operating expenses. By identifying and forecasting your expenses, you can allocate resources more effectively and ensure that you have enough funds to cover your costs.

Tracking expenses is another essential aspect of money management for mobile car washing businesses. Keeping accurate records of your expenses allows you to monitor your spending, identify areas where you can cut costs or increase efficiency, and make informed financial decisions. Consider using accounting software or mobile apps to track expenses digitally, which can streamline the process and provide valuable insights into your business's financial health.

Moreover, managing accounts receivable is crucial for maintaining a healthy cash flow and ensuring timely payment for your services. Establish clear payment terms and policies upfront, and communicate them to your customers before providing services. Send invoices promptly after completing a job, and follow up with customers who have outstanding balances to ensure prompt payment. Consider offering incentives for early payment or implementing late fees for overdue accounts to encourage timely payment and discourage delinquency.

Additionally, managing inventory and supplies efficiently can help mobile car washing operators minimize waste and control costs. Keep track of your inventory levels and reorder supplies as needed to avoid stockouts or excess inventory. Consider negotiating bulk discounts with suppliers or exploring alternative suppliers to reduce costs without sacrificing quality. Implementing inventory management software or systems can help streamline the process and optimize inventory levels for maximum efficiency.

Furthermore, investing in growth is essential for the long-term success of a mobile car washing business. Whether it's expanding your service offerings, investing in marketing and advertising to reach new customers, or upgrading your equipment to improve efficiency and quality, strategic investments can help drive business growth and increase profitability. However, it's essential to carefully evaluate potential investments and consider their potential return on investment (ROI) before committing resources.

Finally, building an emergency fund is a prudent money management strategy for mobile car washing businesses. Unexpected expenses or downturns in business can arise at any time, so having a financial cushion in place can help mitigate the impact of unforeseen challenges and ensure that your business remains resilient and adaptable. Aim to set aside a portion of your revenue each month to build up your emergency fund gradually over time.

In conclusion, effective money management is essential for the success and sustainability of a mobile car washing business. By creating a detailed budget, tracking expenses, managing accounts receivable, optimizing inventory and supplies, investing in growth, and building an emergency fund, mobile car washing operators can optimize cash flow, minimize expenses, and maximize profitability. By implementing these money management strategies, entrepreneurs can position their businesses for long-term success and achieve their financial goals.

Creating a Competitive Business Model

Innovative Strategies: Crafting a Competitive Business Model for Your Mobile Car Washing Service

Crafting a competitive business model is essential for success in the mobile car washing industry, where competition can be fierce and customer expectations are high. By implementing innovative strategies and leveraging unique selling points, mobile car washing operators can differentiate their businesses and gain a competitive edge in the market.

One key aspect of creating a competitive business model is identifying and understanding your target market. Conduct market research to identify customer demographics, preferences, and pain points. Are you targeting busy professionals who value convenience, environmentally conscious consumers who prioritize eco-friendly practices, or luxury car owners who demand premium service? By understanding your target market's needs and preferences, you can tailor your services and marketing efforts to better meet their expectations and stand out from the competition.

Moreover, offering a unique value proposition can help differentiate your mobile car washing business from competitors. Consider what sets your service apart from others in the market. Do you offer eco-friendly cleaning products and water-saving techniques? Do you provide additional services such as interior detailing or scratch removal? Highlighting these unique selling points can help attract customers and position your business as a preferred choice in the market.

Additionally, providing exceptional customer service is crucial for building a competitive business model. Mobile car washing operators should strive to deliver a superior customer experience at every touchpoint, from scheduling appointments to completing the job. Prompt communication, professionalism, attention to detail, and going above and beyond to exceed customer expectations can help build loyalty and generate positive word-of-mouth referrals, ultimately driving business growth.

Furthermore, pricing your services competitively can help attract customers and win market share. Research competitors' pricing and industry standards to ensure that your pricing is competitive while still allowing you to cover your costs and generate a profit.

Consider offering package deals, discounts for regular customers, or loyalty rewards programs to incentivize repeat business and encourage customer retention.

Another important aspect of creating a competitive business model is optimizing operational efficiency. Mobile car washing operators should streamline processes and workflows to minimize downtime, maximize productivity, and deliver services efficiently. Investing in high-quality equipment, implementing standardized procedures, and leveraging technology such as scheduling software or mobile payment solutions can help improve efficiency and enhance the overall customer experience.

Furthermore, building strong partnerships and collaborations can enhance your mobile car washing business's competitiveness. Partnering with local businesses, such as auto dealerships, car rental agencies, or corporate offices, can help expand your customer base and generate consistent business opportunities. Additionally, collaborating with suppliers or industry associations can provide access to resources, networking opportunities, and industry insights that can help fuel business growth and success.

Lastly, staying adaptable and responsive to market changes and customer feedback is essential for maintaining a competitive edge in the mobile car washing industry. Monitor industry trends, customer preferences, and competitor activities to identify opportunities for innovation and improvement. Solicit feedback from customers regularly and use it to refine your services, address pain points, and stay ahead of the competition.

In conclusion, creating a competitive business model is essential for success in the mobile car washing industry. By identifying your target market, offering a unique value proposition, providing exceptional customer service, pricing competitively, optimizing operational efficiency, building strong partnerships, and staying adaptable, mobile car washing operators can differentiate their businesses and gain a competitive edge in the market. By implementing these strategies, entrepreneurs can position their mobile car washing businesses for long-term success and growth.

Services Menu

Offering the Best: Designing a Comprehensive Services Menu for Your Mobile Car Washing Business

Creating a comprehensive services menu is crucial for mobile car washing businesses to attract customers and meet their diverse needs. A well-crafted menu not only showcases the range of services offered but also helps customers understand the value proposition of your business. From basic wash packages to premium detailing services, designing a services menu requires careful consideration of customer preferences, market trends, and business objectives.

At the heart of any mobile car washing services menu are the basic wash packages. These packages typically include exterior cleaning services such as washing, drying, and tire dressing. Basic wash packages are ideal for customers looking for a quick and affordable way to keep their vehicles clean and presentable. Offering multiple levels of basic wash packages, such as standard, deluxe, and premium options, allows customers to choose the level of service that best fits their budget and needs.

In addition to basic wash packages, mobile car washing businesses may offer a range of add-on services to enhance the customer experience and generate additional revenue. Add-on services can include interior cleaning, vacuuming, window cleaning, waxing, polishing, and tire shine treatments. By upselling these add-on services, mobile car washing operators can increase the average transaction value and provide customers with a more comprehensive cleaning experience.

Furthermore, premium detailing services can help mobile car washing businesses attract customers who demand the highest level of care and attention to detail for their vehicles. Premium detailing services typically include deep cleaning and restoration treatments for both the interior and exterior of the vehicle, such as paint correction, upholstery shampooing, leather conditioning, and engine bay cleaning. Offering premium detailing services can help mobile car washing businesses differentiate themselves from competitors and appeal to discerning customers who are willing to pay a premium for quality service.

Moreover, mobile car washing businesses may offer specialty services to target specific customer segments or address niche market needs. For example, offering eco-friendly cleaning options using biodegradable products and water-saving techniques can appeal to environmentally conscious customers. Additionally, offering fleet washing services for businesses with multiple vehicles or mobile detailing services for events and special occasions can provide additional revenue streams and business opportunities.

Furthermore, providing convenient scheduling options and flexible service packages can help mobile car washing businesses attract and retain customers. Offering online booking and scheduling options, as well as subscription-based service plans, can make it easier for customers to schedule appointments and ensure consistent business for the mobile car washing operator. Additionally, offering discounts for regular customers or loyalty rewards programs can incentivize repeat business and encourage customer loyalty.

In conclusion, designing a comprehensive services menu is essential for mobile car washing businesses to attract customers, meet their diverse needs, and maximize revenue potential. By offering a range of basic wash packages, add-on services, premium detailing options, specialty services, and convenient scheduling options, mobile car washing operators can differentiate themselves from competitors and provide customers with a customized and exceptional cleaning experience. By continually evaluating customer feedback and market trends, mobile car washing businesses can refine their services menu to stay relevant and competitive in the dynamic automotive services industry.

Pricing Strategy

Finding the Right Price: Crafting a Successful Pricing Strategy for Your Mobile Car Washing Service

Setting the right pricing strategy is crucial for the success of any business, including mobile car washing services. A well-thought-out pricing strategy not only ensures profitability but also attracts customers, maintains competitiveness, and reflects the value of the services provided. From considering costs and market dynamics to understanding customer perceptions, crafting a successful pricing strategy requires careful analysis and strategic decision-making.

One approach to pricing mobile car washing services is cost-based pricing, which involves calculating the costs associated with providing the service and adding a markup to determine the selling price. Costs to consider include labor, materials, equipment, vehicle expenses, insurance, permits, and overhead costs such as marketing and administration. By understanding and accurately estimating these costs, mobile car washing operators can ensure that their prices cover expenses and generate a reasonable profit margin.

Another pricing strategy for mobile car washing services is value-based pricing, which focuses on the perceived value of the service to the customer rather than the cost of providing it. Value-based pricing takes into account factors such as convenience, quality, reliability, and customer service when determining pricing. By emphasizing the unique value proposition of their services and aligning prices with customer perceptions of value, mobile car washing operators can justify higher prices and differentiate themselves from competitors.

Furthermore, competitive pricing involves analyzing competitors' pricing and positioning your prices relative to theirs. Mobile car washing operators should research competitors' pricing in their local market and assess how their services compare in terms of quality, convenience, and features. Pricing slightly below competitors' prices can help attract price-sensitive customers and gain market share, while pricing slightly above competitors' prices may signal higher quality or premium service offerings.

Moreover, dynamic pricing involves adjusting prices based on market demand, seasonality, and other external factors. Mobile car washing operators may offer discounts or promotions during off-peak hours or slow seasons to incentivize business and generate revenue during periods of low demand. Additionally, dynamic pricing strategies such as surge pricing or peak pricing can help maximize revenue during times of high demand, such as weekends or holidays.

In addition to setting base prices for standard services, mobile car washing operators may offer tiered pricing or package deals to provide customers with options and incentives for upselling. Tiered pricing involves offering multiple levels of service at different price points, allowing customers to choose the level of service that best fits their needs and budget. Package deals, such as bundling multiple services together for a discounted price, can encourage customers to purchase additional services and increase the average transaction value.

Furthermore, transparent pricing and clear communication are essential for building trust and credibility with customers. Mobile car washing operators should clearly communicate prices and service offerings upfront, avoiding hidden fees or surprises. Providing detailed information about the services included in each package, as well as any add-on options and pricing, can help customers make informed decisions and feel confident in their purchasing choices.

In conclusion, crafting a successful pricing strategy for a mobile car washing service requires consideration of costs, value, competition, market dynamics, and customer perceptions. By implementing a thoughtful pricing strategy that aligns with the unique value proposition of their services and meets the needs and preferences of their target market, mobile car washing operators can attract customers, maximize profitability, and build a successful and sustainable business. By continuously evaluating and refining their pricing strategy based on feedback and market conditions, mobile car washing operators can adapt to changing dynamics and maintain competitiveness in the dynamic automotive services industry.

Unique Selling Proposition

Stand Out in the Crowd: Developing a Unique Selling Proposition for Your Mobile Car Washing Service

In a competitive market like the mobile car washing industry, having a unique selling proposition (USP) is essential for attracting customers, differentiating your business from competitors, and ultimately driving success. A USP is what sets your mobile car washing service apart from others in the market and communicates the value you offer to customers. By identifying and leveraging your USP, you can effectively market your business and capture the attention of potential customers.

One potential USP for a mobile car washing service is convenience. Mobile car washing operators bring the service directly to customers' locations, saving them time and hassle by eliminating the need to travel to a physical car wash facility. Highlighting the convenience of your service, such as offering flexible scheduling options, on-demand service, and the ability to wash cars at home or work, can attract busy customers who value convenience and are willing to pay a premium for it.

Moreover, emphasizing the quality and professionalism of your service can be a powerful USP. Mobile car washing operators who prioritize high-quality cleaning products, equipment, and techniques can differentiate themselves from competitors who offer inferior service. By providing consistently excellent results, exceptional customer service, and attention to detail, you can build a reputation for quality and reliability that sets your business apart in the market.

Furthermore, eco-friendliness can be a compelling USP for mobile car washing services. Offering environmentally friendly cleaning products, water-saving techniques, and sustainable practices can appeal to environmentally conscious customers who are seeking to minimize their environmental impact. By promoting your eco-friendly approach and highlighting the benefits of choosing a green car washing service, you can attract a niche market of environmentally conscious consumers and differentiate your business from competitors.

In addition to convenience, quality, and eco-friendliness, specialization can also be a unique selling proposition for mobile car washing services. Specializing in niche markets or offering unique services that cater to specific customer needs can help you stand out from competitors. For example, you could specialize in luxury car detailing, commercial fleet washing, or specialty vehicle cleaning such as RVs or boats. By focusing on a specific niche or offering specialized services, you can position your business as a specialist in the industry and attract customers who value expertise and specialized care.

Moreover, offering competitive pricing or value-added incentives can be a compelling USP for mobile car washing services. Providing discounts for regular customers, loyalty rewards programs, package deals, or free add-on services can differentiate your business and attract price-sensitive customers. By offering value-added incentives that go beyond basic cleaning services, you can create a unique and attractive proposition that sets your business apart from competitors.

Additionally, branding and marketing can play a significant role in communicating your USP to customers and differentiating your business in the market. Developing a strong brand identity, logo, and messaging that reflects your unique value proposition can help build brand recognition and loyalty. Leveraging digital marketing channels such as social media, website optimization, and online advertising can help reach potential customers and communicate your USP effectively.

In conclusion, developing a unique selling proposition is essential for success in the competitive mobile car washing industry. By identifying and leveraging your USP, whether it's convenience, quality, eco-friendliness, specialization, competitive pricing, or value-added incentives, you can differentiate your business from competitors and attract customers who value what you have to offer. By effectively communicating your USP through branding, marketing, and customer engagement, you can build a successful and sustainable mobile car washing business that stands out in the crowd.

Purchasing Appropriate Equipment and Supplies

Investing in the Right Tools: Essential Equipment and Supplies for Your Mobile Car Washing Service

When it comes to operating a successful mobile car washing service, having the appropriate equipment and supplies is essential. Not only does it ensure that you can deliver high-quality cleaning services to your customers, but it also enhances efficiency, professionalism, and customer satisfaction. From pressure washers and cleaning solutions to detailing tools and protective gear, choosing the right equipment and supplies is crucial for the success of your business.

One of the most important pieces of equipment for a mobile car washing service is a reliable pressure washer. Pressure washers come in a variety of sizes and power levels, and choosing the right one depends on factors such as the size of the vehicles you'll be cleaning, the types of surfaces you'll be working on, and your budget. High-pressure washers are ideal for removing tough dirt and grime from vehicle exteriors, while low-pressure washers are better suited for delicate surfaces such as windows and trim.

Additionally, investing in high-quality cleaning solutions is essential for achieving optimal results. Eco-friendly cleaning products are increasingly popular among environmentally conscious consumers and can help differentiate your business from competitors. Look for biodegradable, non-toxic cleaning solutions that are safe for both the environment and the vehicles you'll be cleaning. Additionally, consider offering specialty cleaning products for specific tasks such as removing stains, bugs, or tar from vehicle exteriors.

Furthermore, having the right detailing tools and accessories can make a significant difference in the quality of your work. Detailing brushes, microfiber towels, sponges, and applicators are essential for cleaning and polishing vehicle interiors and exteriors. Investing in high-quality tools made from durable materials ensures that they'll last longer and provide better results. Additionally, consider purchasing accessories such as foam cannons, rotary buffers, and polishing pads to enhance your detailing capabilities and offer additional services to customers.

Moreover, having adequate storage and organization solutions for your equipment and supplies is essential for maintaining a professional appearance and maximizing efficiency. Portable storage containers, toolboxes, and shelving units can help keep your equipment organized and easily accessible while on the go. Additionally, investing in a well-equipped vehicle with built-in storage compartments and racks can streamline the process of transporting and setting up your equipment at job sites.

In addition to equipment, having the appropriate protective gear is essential for ensuring the safety of yourself and your employees. Protective gear such as gloves, safety goggles, and respirators protects against exposure to cleaning chemicals and potential hazards while working. Additionally, investing in ergonomic equipment such as knee pads and back braces can help prevent injuries and reduce fatigue during long hours of work.

Furthermore, staying up-to-date with the latest technology and innovations in the industry can help you stay competitive and provide better service to your customers. Keep an eye out for advancements in equipment such as water-saving technologies, eco-friendly cleaning solutions, and digital tools for scheduling and invoicing. By embracing technology and innovation, you can enhance your efficiency, reduce costs, and differentiate your business in the market.

In conclusion, purchasing appropriate equipment and supplies is essential for the success of your mobile car washing service. From pressure washers and cleaning solutions to detailing tools and protective gear, investing in the right equipment ensures that you can deliver high-quality cleaning services to your customers efficiently and professionally. By choosing equipment and supplies that meet your needs, investing in storage and organization solutions, prioritizing safety, and staying up-to-date with industry advancements, you can set your mobile car washing business up for success and provide exceptional service to your customers.

Equipment Selection

Selecting the Right Tools: A Guide to Equipment Selection for Your Mobile Car Washing Service

When it comes to running a mobile car washing service, choosing the right equipment is paramount to success. The equipment you select will directly impact the quality of your service, efficiency of your operations, and overall customer satisfaction. From pressure washers and water tanks to detailing tools and safety equipment, each piece of equipment plays a crucial role in delivering exceptional results while on the go.

One of the most essential pieces of equipment for a mobile car washing service is the pressure washer. Pressure washers come in various sizes, power capacities, and features, so selecting the right one depends on the scope of your operations and types of vehicles you'll be washing. For instance, if you primarily wash large vehicles like trucks and SUVs, you may need a high-powered pressure washer with a larger water flow rate and PSI (pounds per square inch) capability. Conversely, if you focus on smaller cars or delicate surfaces, a lower-powered pressure washer with adjustable settings may be more suitable to avoid causing damage.

Additionally, having a reliable water source is crucial for mobile car washing operations. While some operators may opt for connecting to clients' water supplies, others prefer the convenience of carrying their own water tanks. When selecting water tanks, consider factors such as capacity, portability, and durability. Look for tanks made from high-quality materials that can withstand transportation and provide sufficient water supply for a day's worth of work.

Furthermore, investing in high-quality cleaning solutions is essential for achieving optimal results and ensuring customer satisfaction. Choose eco-friendly cleaning products that are safe for both the environment and the vehicles you'll be cleaning. Consider products that are biodegradable, non-toxic, and free from harsh chemicals that could potentially damage vehicle surfaces or harm the environment. Additionally, having a variety of cleaning solutions for different tasks, such as degreasers, wheel cleaners, and interior cleaners, allows you to address various cleaning needs effectively.

Moreover, having the right detailing tools and accessories can make a significant difference in the quality of your work. Detailing brushes, microfiber towels, sponges, and applicators are essential for cleaning and polishing vehicle surfaces. Invest in high-quality tools made from durable materials to ensure longevity and optimal performance.

Additionally, consider accessories such as foam cannons, rotary buffers, and polishing pads to enhance your detailing capabilities and offer premium services to your clients.

In addition to cleaning equipment, investing in safety gear is crucial to protect yourself and your employees while on the job. Safety equipment such as gloves, safety goggles, and respirators shields against exposure to cleaning chemicals and potential hazards. Additionally, ergonomic equipment such as knee pads and back braces can help prevent injuries and reduce fatigue during long hours of work. Prioritizing safety not only protects your team but also contributes to a professional image and instills confidence in your clients.

Furthermore, staying up-to-date with technological advancements can help you stay competitive and provide better service to your clients. Keep an eye out for innovations in equipment such as water-saving technologies, eco-friendly cleaning solutions, and digital tools for scheduling and invoicing. Embracing technology can enhance efficiency, reduce costs, and differentiate your business from competitors in the market.

In conclusion, selecting the right equipment is crucial for the success of your mobile car washing service. From pressure washers and water tanks to cleaning solutions, detailing tools, and safety equipment, each piece of equipment plays a vital role in delivering exceptional service and customer satisfaction. By investing in high-quality equipment, prioritizing safety, and staying informed about industry advancements, you can set your mobile car washing business up for success and provide top-notch service to your clients.

Sustainable Cleaning Products

Embracing Eco-Friendly Solutions: Sustainable Cleaning Products for Your Mobile Car Washing Service

In today's environmentally conscious world, businesses of all kinds are increasingly turning to sustainable practices, and the mobile car washing industry is no exception. As awareness of environmental issues grows, customers are seeking out eco-friendly alternatives, including cleaning products that minimize harm to the environment while still delivering excellent results. Transitioning to sustainable cleaning products not only benefits the planet but also enhances your business's reputation, attracts eco-conscious customers, and contributes to a healthier, greener future.

One of the primary considerations when selecting sustainable cleaning products for your mobile car washing service is choosing products that are biodegradable. Biodegradable products are designed to break down into harmless substances when they come into contact with water or other natural elements, reducing their impact on the environment. Look for cleaning solutions that are certified as biodegradable by reputable third-party organizations to ensure their effectiveness and environmental safety.

Moreover, opt for cleaning products that are free from harsh chemicals such as phosphates, ammonia, and chlorine. These chemicals can be harmful to aquatic life, soil health, and human health, especially when they're washed away into waterways or absorbed into the ground. Instead, choose eco-friendly cleaning solutions that are formulated with natural, plant-based ingredients and are free from toxic chemicals that can harm the environment or pose health risks to your customers and employees.

Furthermore, consider the packaging of the cleaning products you use and opt for options that minimize waste and are recyclable or biodegradable. Look for products that come in recyclable containers or packaging made from recycled materials to reduce your carbon footprint and minimize landfill waste. Additionally, choose concentrated cleaning solutions that require less packaging and transportation, further reducing your environmental impact and lowering your overall costs.

In addition to being environmentally friendly, sustainable cleaning products should also be effective at removing dirt, grime, and grease from vehicle surfaces. Look for products that are specifically formulated for automotive use and are capable of delivering high-quality results without compromising on performance. Test different eco-friendly cleaning solutions to ensure they meet your standards for cleaning power and effectiveness before incorporating them into your mobile car washing service.

Furthermore, consider the water usage and wastewater disposal practices associated with the cleaning products you use. Opt for products that require minimal water usage and produce less wastewater runoff, helping to conserve water resources and reduce pollution. Additionally, implement proper wastewater disposal procedures to prevent contaminated water from entering storm drains or natural waterways, minimizing the environmental impact of your operations.

Moreover, educate your customers about the benefits of using sustainable cleaning products and encourage them to make environmentally friendly choices. Highlighting your commitment to sustainability and offering eco-friendly cleaning options can attract environmentally conscious customers who value businesses that prioritize environmental stewardship. Additionally, provide information about the environmental benefits of sustainable cleaning products and the importance of protecting the planet for future generations.

In conclusion, embracing sustainable cleaning products is essential for mobile car washing services looking to minimize their environmental impact and meet the growing demand for eco-friendly alternatives. By choosing biodegradable, chemical-free products, minimizing packaging waste, prioritizing effectiveness, and educating customers about the benefits of sustainability, mobile car washing operators can reduce their environmental footprint, attract eco-conscious customers, and contribute to a cleaner, greener future. By incorporating sustainable practices into their operations, mobile car washing services can demonstrate their commitment to environmental stewardship and differentiate themselves in the market.

Inventory Management

Efficient Inventory Management for Mobile Car Washing Services

Effective inventory management is crucial for the smooth operation and success of any business, including mobile car washing services. Properly managing inventory ensures that you have the necessary supplies on hand to meet customer demand, minimize waste, and optimize profitability. From cleaning solutions and detailing tools to equipment parts and safety gear, implementing efficient inventory management practices can streamline operations and enhance customer satisfaction.

One of the first steps in inventory management for mobile car washing services is conducting a thorough inventory assessment. Take stock of all the supplies, equipment, and materials you use in your operations, including cleaning solutions, detailing tools, equipment parts, safety gear, and administrative supplies. Determine the quantity of each item you currently have on hand, its location, and its condition. This information forms the foundation for effective inventory management and helps identify areas for improvement.

Moreover, establishing minimum and maximum stock levels for each inventory item can help prevent stockouts and overstocking. Determine the optimal quantity of each item to keep on hand based on factors such as demand, lead time, storage space, and budget constraints. Set minimum stock levels to ensure that you never run out of essential items, while setting maximum stock levels helps prevent excess inventory and ties up valuable resources unnecessarily.

Furthermore, implementing a reliable inventory tracking system is essential for keeping track of inventory levels, movements, and usage. Consider using inventory management software or mobile apps that allow you to track inventory in real-time, automate reordering processes, and generate reports for analysis. Barcode scanners, RFID tags, and other automated tracking technologies can also streamline inventory management and reduce errors associated with manual tracking methods.

In addition to tracking inventory levels, monitoring inventory turnover rates can help identify slow-moving items or areas of inefficiency. Inventory turnover measures how quickly inventory is sold or used within a specific period, such as a month or a year. High turnover rates indicate efficient inventory management and healthy sales, while low turnover rates may signal excess inventory or poor demand forecasting. Analyzing inventory turnover rates allows you to adjust ordering quantities, identify obsolete inventory, and optimize inventory levels for maximum efficiency.

Moreover, establishing clear inventory management procedures and protocols helps ensure consistency and accuracy in inventory management practices. Develop standardized processes for receiving, storing, picking, and replenishing inventory items to minimize errors and streamline operations. Train employees on proper inventory management techniques and procedures to ensure compliance and foster a culture of accountability and efficiency.

Additionally, conducting regular audits and reviews of inventory practices can help identify areas for improvement and optimize inventory management processes. Perform physical inventory counts periodically to reconcile inventory records with actual inventory levels and identify discrepancies. Analyze inventory data and performance metrics to identify trends, patterns, and opportunities for optimization, such as identifying slow-moving items, reducing stockouts, or improving order accuracy.

Furthermore, establishing relationships with reliable suppliers and vendors is essential for ensuring a steady supply of inventory items and maintaining quality standards. Research suppliers carefully, considering factors such as price, quality, reliability, and delivery times. Negotiate favorable terms and agreements with suppliers to secure competitive pricing, minimize lead times, and ensure consistent supply chain performance.

In conclusion, efficient inventory management is essential for the success and profitability of mobile car washing services. By conducting thorough inventory assessments, establishing optimal stock levels, implementing reliable tracking systems, monitoring turnover rates, establishing clear procedures, conducting regular audits, and fostering relationships with suppliers, mobile car washing operators can streamline operations, optimize inventory levels, and enhance customer satisfaction. Effective inventory management allows mobile car washing services to meet customer demand, minimize waste, and maximize profitability, ultimately positioning them for long-term success and growth.

Setting Up Your Mobile Car Wash Van

Optimizing Your Mobile Car Wash Van for Efficiency and Effectiveness

Setting up your mobile car wash van is a crucial step in establishing a successful and efficient operation for your mobile car washing service. The layout, organization, and equipment placement within your van can significantly impact your ability to deliver high-quality service, maximize productivity, and provide an exceptional customer experience. By carefully planning and optimizing your mobile car wash van setup, you can streamline operations, minimize downtime, and position your business for success.

First and foremost, consider the layout and organization of your mobile car wash van to maximize efficiency and functionality. Designate specific areas within the van for different tasks, such as cleaning, detailing, storage, and equipment maintenance. Ensure that commonly used items and tools are easily accessible, while less frequently used items are stored securely to minimize clutter and optimize workspace.

Moreover, invest in storage solutions such as shelving units, cabinets, and storage bins to keep your van organized and clutter-free. Utilize vertical space efficiently to maximize storage capacity while keeping essential items within reach. Consider installing hooks, racks, and holders for hanging tools, hoses, and cleaning supplies to prevent them from rolling around or becoming tangled during transit.

Furthermore, strategically place equipment and machinery within your mobile car wash van to optimize workflow and minimize setup time at job sites. Position pressure washers, water tanks, and cleaning solutions in easily accessible locations near the rear or side doors for quick setup and teardown. Arrange detailing tools, brushes, towels, and other accessories in designated compartments or storage bins for easy access and efficient use during cleaning and detailing tasks.

In addition to equipment placement, consider installing additional features and amenities in your mobile car wash van to enhance comfort, convenience, and productivity. Install a retractable awning or canopy to provide shade and protection from the elements during outdoor cleaning sessions. Consider adding a water filtration system or deionizer to purify water and minimize water spots on vehicle surfaces.

Moreover, invest in ergonomic seating and workspace configurations to minimize fatigue and discomfort during long hours of work. Consider installing a comfortable captain's chair or ergonomic seat cushion for the driver's seat, as well as adjustable seats or benches for workstations within the van. Ensure that work surfaces are at a comfortable height and angle to prevent strain and promote proper posture while performing tasks.

Additionally, outfit your mobile car wash van with essential safety features and equipment to protect yourself, your employees, and your customers. Install fire extinguishers, first aid kits, and emergency signage in easily accessible locations within the van. Ensure that all equipment and machinery are properly secured during transit to prevent accidents or injuries.

Furthermore, invest in vehicle maintenance and upkeep to ensure that your mobile car wash van remains in optimal condition and operates reliably. Schedule regular inspections, tune-ups, and servicing for your van to prevent breakdowns and minimize downtime. Keep tires properly inflated, fluids topped off, and brakes and lights in working order to ensure safe operation on the road.

In conclusion, setting up your mobile car wash van is a critical step in establishing a successful and efficient operation for your mobile car washing service. By carefully planning and optimizing the layout, organization, and equipment placement within your van, you can streamline operations, maximize productivity, and provide an exceptional customer experience. Investing in storage solutions, equipment placement, additional features, safety equipment, vehicle maintenance, and upkeep ensures that your mobile car wash van remains efficient, effective, and reliable for years to come.

Buying vs Renting

Deciding between Buying and Renting Equipment for Your Mobile Car Washing Service

When starting a mobile car washing service, one of the key decisions you'll need to make is whether to buy or rent equipment. Each option has its own set of advantages and disadvantages, and the choice depends on factors such as your budget, long-term goals, and specific business needs. By weighing the pros and cons of buying versus renting equipment, you can make an informed decision that best suits your circumstances and sets your business up for success.

Buying equipment offers the advantage of ownership and control over your assets. When you buy equipment outright, you have the flexibility to use it as you see fit, customize it to meet your specific needs, and make modifications or upgrades as necessary. Additionally, owning equipment allows you to build equity in your business and potentially increase its value over time. For mobile car washing services, owning equipment such as pressure washers, water tanks, and detailing tools provides the assurance of reliability and availability whenever needed.

Moreover, buying equipment may be more cost-effective in the long run, especially if you plan to use it frequently or for an extended period. While the initial upfront costs of purchasing equipment may be higher than renting, you avoid ongoing rental fees and expenses, which can add up over time. Additionally, owning equipment allows you to amortize the cost over its useful life and potentially recoup your investment through increased productivity, efficiency, and profitability.

However, buying equipment also comes with certain drawbacks and considerations. The initial capital outlay required to purchase equipment can be significant, especially for high-quality or specialized equipment used in mobile car washing services. Additionally, owning equipment entails ongoing maintenance, repairs, and operating costs, which can add up over time and impact your bottom line. Furthermore, owning equipment ties up capital that could be used for other business expenses or investment opportunities.

On the other hand, renting equipment offers the advantage of flexibility and cost savings, especially for short-term or temporary needs. Renting allows you to access equipment quickly and easily without the need for a large upfront investment. Additionally, renting equipment eliminates the burden of ownership, including maintenance, repairs, and storage, as these responsibilities typically fall on the rental company. For mobile car washing services, renting equipment may be preferable for seasonal or occasional needs, such as peak demand periods or special events.

Moreover, renting equipment allows you to experiment with different types of equipment or try out new technologies without committing to a long-term investment. This flexibility can be advantageous for mobile car washing operators looking to test new services or expand their offerings without the risk of purchasing expensive equipment upfront. Additionally, renting equipment can be a tax-deductible expense for your business, providing potential tax benefits and cost savings.

However, renting equipment also has its limitations and considerations. Rental fees can add up over time, especially if you require equipment on a regular basis or for an extended period. Additionally, renting equipment may limit your access to certain models or features, as rental companies may have a limited selection of available equipment. Furthermore, relying on rented equipment may pose challenges in terms of availability, reliability, and scheduling, especially during peak demand periods or emergencies.

In conclusion, deciding between buying and renting equipment for your mobile car washing service requires careful consideration of your specific business needs, budget, and long-term goals. While buying equipment offers the advantages of ownership, control, and potential cost savings in the long run, renting equipment provides flexibility, convenience, and upfront cost savings, especially for short-term or temporary needs. By weighing the pros and cons of each option and evaluating your circumstances, you can make an informed decision that best serves your business and sets you up for success in the dynamic mobile car washing industry.

Van Customization Options

Transforming Your Mobile Car Wash Van: Customization Options to Consider

When setting up a mobile car washing service, the customization of your van plays a crucial role in enhancing efficiency, productivity, and customer satisfaction. From interior layout and storage solutions to exterior branding and equipment installations, there are numerous customization options available to tailor your van to meet the specific needs of your business. By exploring these customization options, you can create a mobile car wash van that stands out from the competition and delivers exceptional service to your customers.

One of the primary considerations when customizing your mobile car wash van is the interior layout and organization. Designate specific areas within the van for different tasks, such as cleaning, detailing, equipment storage, and administrative work. Consider installing shelving units, cabinets, and storage bins to keep your van organized and clutter-free, maximizing workspace and efficiency. Utilize vertical space effectively to maximize storage capacity while keeping essential items within easy reach during mobile car washing operations.

Moreover, outfitting your mobile car wash van with the necessary equipment and machinery is essential for delivering high-quality service on the go. Consider installing a powerful pressure washer, water tanks, and storage compartments for cleaning solutions and detailing tools. Customize the layout and placement of equipment to optimize workflow and minimize setup time at job sites. Additionally, consider installing specialized equipment such as water filtration systems, deionizers, or steam cleaners to enhance your service offerings and differentiate your business from competitors.

Furthermore, branding and exterior customization can help promote your mobile car washing service and attract potential customers while on the road. Invest in professional vehicle wraps or decals featuring your business logo, name, and contact information to create a visually appealing and recognizable presence. Choose eye-catching colors and designs that reflect your brand identity and convey professionalism and trustworthiness to customers. Additionally, consider adding signage or banners to the exterior of your van to advertise special promotions, discounts, or services.

In addition to interior layout and branding, consider incorporating additional features and amenities to enhance comfort, convenience, and productivity. Install a retractable awning or canopy to provide shade and protection from the elements during outdoor cleaning sessions. Consider adding interior lighting, ventilation, and climate control systems to create a comfortable and ergonomic workspace for you and your employees. Additionally, outfit your van with ergonomic seating, work surfaces, and storage solutions to minimize fatigue and promote efficiency during long hours of work.

Moreover, investing in safety features and equipment is essential for protecting yourself, your employees, and your customers while on the job. Install fire extinguishers, first aid kits, and emergency signage in easily accessible locations within the van. Ensure that all equipment and machinery are properly secured during transit to prevent accidents or injuries. Additionally, consider installing backup cameras, alarms, or GPS tracking systems to enhance vehicle security and driver safety while on the road.

In conclusion, customizing your mobile car wash van is a critical step in establishing a successful and efficient operation for your mobile car washing service. By carefully planning and implementing interior layout, equipment installations, branding, and safety features, you can create a mobile car wash van that meets the specific needs of your business and sets you apart from the competition. Investing in customization options that enhance efficiency, productivity, and customer satisfaction ultimately positions your mobile car washing service for long-term success and growth in the competitive market.

Daily Operations and Maintenance

Efficient Daily Operations and Maintenance Practices for Your Mobile Car Washing Service

Running a successful mobile car washing service requires more than just providing excellent cleaning and detailing services to your customers. It also involves efficiently managing daily operations and performing regular maintenance to ensure that your business runs smoothly and your equipment remains in optimal condition. By implementing effective daily operations and maintenance practices, you can enhance productivity, prolong the lifespan of your equipment, and deliver exceptional service to your clients.

One of the key aspects of daily operations for a mobile car washing service is scheduling and route planning. Efficiently organizing your daily schedule and mapping out your routes helps minimize travel time between job sites, maximize the number of appointments you can handle in a day, and reduce fuel consumption and vehicle wear and tear. Utilize scheduling software or mobile apps to manage appointments, track customer locations, and optimize routes based on factors such as traffic patterns and job requirements.

Moreover, maintaining cleanliness and organization within your mobile car wash van is essential for creating a professional and efficient workspace. Take time at the end of each workday to clean and tidy up your van, disposing of trash, wiping down surfaces, and organizing equipment and supplies. Regularly inspect and inventory your inventory items to ensure that you have an adequate supply for upcoming appointments and replenish as needed to avoid stockouts or delays.

Furthermore, performing routine maintenance on your equipment is crucial for ensuring reliability, safety, and optimal performance. Develop a maintenance schedule for each piece of equipment and machinery used in your mobile car washing service, including pressure washers, water tanks, hoses, and detailing tools. Follow manufacturer recommendations for maintenance tasks such as lubrication, filter changes, and inspection of hoses and connections. Additionally, keep records of maintenance activities and inspections to track equipment performance and identify potential issues early.

In addition to equipment maintenance, regular vehicle maintenance is essential for keeping your mobile car wash van in top condition. Schedule routine inspections and servicing for your van, including oil changes, tire rotations, brake checks, and fluid top-ups. Keep an eye out for signs of wear and tear, such as unusual noises, vibrations, or fluid leaks, and address them promptly to prevent further damage or breakdowns. Additionally, ensure that your van is clean and presentable both inside and out, as it serves as a mobile billboard for your business.

Moreover, maintaining communication and relationships with your customers is vital for fostering loyalty and repeat business. Follow up with customers after appointments to ensure satisfaction with your services and address any concerns or issues promptly. Collect feedback from customers to identify areas for improvement and implement changes to enhance the customer experience. Additionally, use customer relationship management (CRM) software or tools to track customer preferences, scheduling preferences, and appointment history for personalized service.

Furthermore, staying informed about industry trends, regulations, and best practices is essential for staying competitive and compliant in the mobile car washing industry. Stay connected with industry associations, forums, and publications to stay up-to-date on the latest developments and innovations. Additionally, invest in ongoing training and professional development for yourself and your employees to stay current on new technologies, techniques, and safety protocols.

In conclusion, efficient daily operations and maintenance practices are essential for the success and sustainability of your mobile car washing service. By implementing effective scheduling and route planning, maintaining cleanliness and organization within your van, performing routine maintenance on your equipment and vehicle, communicating with customers, and staying informed about industry trends, you can enhance productivity, prolong equipment lifespan, and deliver exceptional service to your clients. Prioritizing daily operations and maintenance ensures that your mobile car washing business operates smoothly, efficiently, and profitably in the competitive market.

Hiring and Training Staff

Building a Competent Team: Hiring and Training Staff for Your Mobile Car Washing Service

In the mobile car washing service industry, hiring and training competent staff is crucial for delivering high-quality service and maintaining customer satisfaction. From cleaning technicians and detailers to administrative staff and customer service representatives, each member of your team plays a vital role in the success of your business. By implementing effective hiring and training practices, you can build a skilled and dedicated team that contributes to the growth and reputation of your mobile car washing service.

When hiring staff for your mobile car washing service, it's essential to look for individuals who possess the necessary skills, experience, and attributes to excel in their roles. Seek candidates with previous experience in automotive detailing, cleaning, or customer service, as they will already have a solid foundation of knowledge and skills relevant to the industry. Additionally, look for candidates who demonstrate reliability, attention to detail, and a strong work ethic, as these qualities are essential for delivering exceptional service to your customers.

Moreover, consider conducting thorough interviews and screening processes to assess candidates' qualifications, experience, and fit for your business. Ask probing questions about their previous work experience, relevant skills, and problem-solving abilities to gauge their suitability for the role. Additionally, consider conducting practical assessments or skills tests to evaluate candidates' proficiency in tasks such as cleaning, detailing, and customer interaction. Look for candidates who demonstrate enthusiasm, adaptability, and a willingness to learn and grow within your organization.

Furthermore, when training new staff for your mobile car washing service, it's essential to provide comprehensive and hands-on instruction to ensure that they understand their roles and responsibilities fully. Develop a structured training program that covers essential topics such as equipment operation, cleaning techniques, safety protocols, customer service standards, and company policies and procedures. Provide opportunities for new hires to shadow experienced team members, observe demonstrations, and practice hands-on tasks to reinforce learning and build confidence.

In addition to technical skills training, emphasize the importance of professionalism, customer service, and teamwork in delivering exceptional service to your clients. Train your staff on effective communication techniques, conflict resolution strategies, and customer interaction skills to ensure positive interactions and experiences for your customers. Additionally, foster a culture of teamwork, collaboration, and mutual respect among your staff to promote a supportive and productive work environment.

Moreover, invest in ongoing training and professional development opportunities for your staff to keep their skills sharp and up-to-date with industry trends and best practices. Encourage staff members to participate in workshops, seminars, and certification programs related to automotive detailing, customer service, and safety. Additionally, provide regular feedback, coaching, and performance evaluations to help your staff identify areas for improvement and grow professionally within your organization.

Furthermore, recognize and reward outstanding performance and contributions from your staff to boost morale, motivation, and job satisfaction. Implement incentives, bonuses, or recognition programs to acknowledge exemplary performance, exceed customer expectations, or achieve specific goals. Additionally, create opportunities for career advancement and growth within your organization, such as promotions, leadership roles, or additional responsibilities, to encourage loyalty and commitment among your team members.

In conclusion, hiring and training staff for your mobile car washing service is essential for delivering high-quality service, maintaining customer satisfaction, and building a successful business. By recruiting qualified candidates, providing comprehensive training and support, fostering a culture of professionalism and teamwork, and investing in ongoing development opportunities, you can build a skilled and dedicated team that contributes to the growth and reputation of your mobile car washing service. Prioritizing hiring and training practices ensures that your business operates smoothly, efficiently, and profitably in the competitive market.

Recruitment Strategies

Effective Recruitment Strategies for Your Mobile Car Washing Service

Recruiting the right talent is essential for the success and growth of any business, including mobile car washing services. With the right team in place, you can deliver high-quality service, exceed customer expectations, and build a strong reputation in the industry. However, finding and attracting qualified candidates can be a challenge, especially in a competitive job market. By implementing effective recruitment strategies tailored to the unique needs of your mobile car washing service, you can attract top talent and build a skilled and dedicated team.

One effective recruitment strategy for mobile car washing services is leveraging online job boards and recruitment platforms to reach a broader audience of potential candidates. Post job openings on popular job search websites, industry-specific forums, and social media platforms to increase visibility and attract candidates with relevant skills and experience. Additionally, consider utilizing niche job boards or forums specifically tailored to the automotive industry to target candidates with a passion for cars and detailing.

Moreover, consider tapping into your existing network and reaching out to industry professionals, trade schools, and vocational programs to identify potential candidates for your mobile car washing service. Attend job fairs, career expos, and networking events to connect with job seekers and promote opportunities within your organization. Additionally, consider offering internships, apprenticeships, or work-study programs to attract candidates who are eager to gain hands-on experience and learn the ropes of the industry.

Furthermore, consider incentivizing employee referrals as a recruitment strategy for your mobile car washing service. Encourage your existing team members to refer qualified candidates for open positions and reward them for successful referrals. Offer bonuses, incentives, or other rewards for referrals that result in successful hires, motivating your employees to actively participate in the recruitment process and tap into their networks to find top talent.

In addition to traditional recruitment methods, consider utilizing digital marketing and branding strategies to attract potential candidates to your mobile car washing service. Develop a compelling employer brand that highlights the unique benefits and opportunities of working for your organization, such as flexible schedules, competitive wages, and opportunities for career growth. Create engaging and informative content, such as blog posts, videos, and social media posts, that showcase your company culture, values, and the rewarding nature of the work.

Moreover, consider offering attractive incentives and benefits to entice candidates to join your mobile car washing service. Offer competitive wages, performance bonuses, and incentives such as employee discounts or perks to attract top talent and retain skilled employees. Additionally, consider offering benefits such as health insurance, retirement plans, and paid time off to enhance your compensation package and differentiate your mobile car washing service as an employer of choice.

Furthermore, consider partnering with local schools, community organizations, and workforce development agencies to recruit candidates from underserved or underrepresented populations. Offer training programs, apprenticeships, or job placement services to help individuals gain valuable skills and experience in the automotive industry and secure employment opportunities with your mobile car washing service. By actively engaging with the community and supporting workforce development initiatives, you can attract diverse talent and contribute to the economic growth and prosperity of your local community.

In conclusion, effective recruitment strategies are essential for attracting top talent and building a skilled and dedicated team for your mobile car washing service. By leveraging online job boards, networking opportunities, employee referrals, digital marketing, and branding strategies, you can reach a broader audience of potential candidates and position your organization as an employer of choice in the competitive job market. Additionally, offering attractive incentives, benefits, and opportunities for career growth can help attract and retain skilled employees who are passionate about the automotive industry and committed to delivering exceptional service to your customers.

Training Manuals and Procedures

Developing Effective Training Manuals and Procedures for Your Mobile Car Washing Service

Training manuals and procedures are essential tools for ensuring consistency, efficiency, and quality in your mobile car washing service. They provide a comprehensive guide for new hires to learn the necessary skills, techniques, and procedures required to perform their roles effectively. Additionally, they serve as a reference resource for existing employees to refresh their knowledge, improve their skills, and maintain service standards. By developing clear, informative, and user-friendly training manuals and procedures, you can empower your team to deliver exceptional service and uphold your brand reputation in the competitive market.

One of the first steps in developing training manuals and procedures for your mobile car washing service is identifying the key areas and tasks that need to be covered. Consider the different roles and responsibilities within your organization, such as cleaning technicians, detailers, customer service representatives, and administrative staff, and outline the specific skills and knowledge required for each role. Additionally, identify the essential tasks and procedures involved in mobile car washing operations, such as vehicle preparation, cleaning techniques, equipment operation, and customer interaction.

Moreover, organize the content of your training manuals and procedures in a logical and easy-to-follow format that facilitates learning and comprehension. Divide the information into sections or chapters based on topics such as equipment operation, cleaning procedures, safety protocols, and customer service standards. Use clear headings, subheadings, and bullet points to break down complex information into manageable chunks and enhance readability. Additionally, include visual aids such as diagrams, illustrations, and photographs to complement written instructions and reinforce key concepts.

Furthermore, tailor your training manuals and procedures to the specific needs and requirements of your mobile car washing service. Customize the content to reflect your company's unique processes, equipment, and service offerings. Incorporate real-life examples, case studies, and scenarios to make the training materials relevant and relatable to employees' day-to-day responsibilities. Additionally, include tips, tricks, and best practices based on your team's collective experience to enhance the effectiveness of the training program.

In addition to written materials, consider incorporating hands-on training and practical demonstrations into your training program to reinforce learning and build practical skills. Provide opportunities for new hires to observe experienced team members in action, ask questions, and practice hands-on tasks under supervision. Additionally, offer opportunities for role-playing, simulated scenarios, and on-the-job training to help employees gain confidence and proficiency in their roles.

Moreover, regularly review and update your training manuals and procedures to reflect changes in technology, equipment, regulations, and best practices. Keep abreast of industry developments and incorporate new information, techniques, and technologies into your training materials as needed. Additionally, solicit feedback from employees on the effectiveness of the training program and make adjustments based on their input and suggestions. By continuously improving and evolving your training program, you can ensure that your team remains knowledgeable, skilled, and adaptable in the dynamic mobile car washing industry.

Furthermore, ensure that your training manuals and procedures are easily accessible to all employees and readily available for reference as needed. Distribute printed copies or digital versions of the training materials to all team members and provide access to an online portal or shared drive where they can access updated versions and additional resources. Encourage employees to use the training materials as a reference resource and refer to them regularly to refresh their knowledge and skills.

In conclusion, developing effective training manuals and procedures is essential for ensuring consistency, efficiency, and quality in your mobile car washing service. By identifying key areas and tasks, organizing content in a user-friendly format, tailoring materials to your specific needs, incorporating hands-on training, regularly updating materials, and ensuring accessibility, you can empower your team to deliver exceptional service and uphold your brand reputation in the competitive market. Prioritizing the development of comprehensive and informative training materials ultimately contributes to the success and growth of your mobile car washing service.

Employee Motivation and Retention

Employee Motivation and Retention Strategies in Mobile Car Washing Services

Employee motivation and retention are critical factors in the success of any business, including mobile car washing services. A motivated and engaged workforce is more likely to deliver high-quality service, exceed customer expectations, and contribute to the overall success and growth of the business. Moreover, retaining skilled and experienced employees helps reduce turnover costs, maintain service consistency, and foster a positive work environment. By implementing effective strategies to motivate and retain employees, mobile car washing services can build a loyal and dedicated team that drives success in the competitive market.

One key strategy for motivating and retaining employees in mobile car washing services is recognizing and rewarding their contributions and achievements. Acknowledge and celebrate employees' successes, milestones, and outstanding performance through verbal praise, written commendations, or public recognition. Additionally, consider implementing rewards and incentive programs that offer tangible rewards such as bonuses, gift cards, or additional time off for exceptional performance, exceeding goals, or providing excellent customer service.

Moreover, provide opportunities for professional development and growth to motivate employees and encourage them to invest in their careers with your mobile car washing service. Offer training programs, workshops, seminars, and certifications related to automotive detailing, customer service, safety protocols, and leadership development. Additionally, provide opportunities for advancement and career progression within the organization, such as promotions, leadership roles, or additional responsibilities, to demonstrate your commitment to employees' long-term success and growth.

Furthermore, foster a positive and supportive work environment that promotes teamwork, collaboration, and mutual respect among employees. Encourage open communication, feedback, and idea sharing to create a sense of belonging and ownership among team members. Additionally, provide opportunities for social interaction and team building activities, such as company outings, team lunches, or recreational events, to strengthen relationships and morale within the team.

In addition to recognition and professional development opportunities, offering competitive compensation and benefits packages is essential for attracting and retaining top talent in the mobile car washing industry. Conduct regular salary reviews and benchmarking to ensure that your compensation packages remain competitive with industry standards and local market rates. Additionally, offer benefits such as health insurance, retirement plans, paid time off, and employee discounts to enhance the overall value proposition for your employees.

Moreover, prioritize work-life balance and flexibility to accommodate the diverse needs and preferences of your employees. Offer flexible scheduling options, such as part-time, full-time, or seasonal positions, to accommodate employees' personal commitments and preferences. Additionally, consider offering remote work or telecommuting options for administrative roles or tasks that can be performed off-site, providing employees with greater flexibility and autonomy over their work schedules.

Furthermore, solicit feedback and input from employees on a regular basis to understand their needs, concerns, and areas for improvement. Conduct employee surveys, focus groups, or one-on-one meetings to gather feedback on workplace satisfaction, job satisfaction, and areas for improvement. Use this feedback to identify opportunities for enhancement and implement changes or initiatives to address employees' concerns and improve their overall experience working for your mobile car washing service.

In conclusion, employee motivation and retention are essential for the success and sustainability of mobile car washing services. By recognizing and rewarding employees' contributions, providing opportunities for professional development and growth, fostering a positive work environment, offering competitive compensation and benefits packages, prioritizing work-life balance and flexibility, and soliciting feedback and input from employees, mobile car washing services can build a motivated, engaged, and loyal workforce that drives success in the competitive market. Prioritizing employee motivation and retention ultimately contributes to the overall success and growth of the business.

In addition to providing employees with the necessary PPE, mobile car washing services must ensure that PPE is properly maintained, cleaned, and replaced as needed. Inspect PPE regularly for signs of wear, damage, or deterioration, and replace any damaged or expired equipment promptly. Additionally, provide employees with training on the proper use, care, and maintenance of PPE to ensure its effectiveness and longevity. Encourage employees to report any issues or concerns with their PPE so that they can be addressed promptly and appropriately.

Moreover, mobile car washing services should establish clear policies and procedures regarding the use of PPE in the workplace. Communicate expectations to employees regarding when and where PPE should be worn, as well as how to properly don, doff, and adjust PPE for optimal fit and protection. Additionally, provide training on hazard recognition, risk assessment, and emergency procedures to empower employees to make informed decisions about PPE usage in different situations. Regularly review and update policies and procedures to reflect changes in equipment, regulations, or best practices.

In conclusion, Personal Protective Equipment (PPE) plays a vital role in ensuring the safety and well-being of employees in mobile car washing services. By providing employees with appropriate PPE and ensuring its proper use, mobile car washing services can protect against chemical exposure, physical hazards, environmental conditions, and other risks encountered on the job. Moreover, by establishing clear policies and procedures, providing training, and maintaining PPE, mobile car washing services can create a safe working environment and prevent accidents or injuries in the workplace. Prioritizing the use of PPE ultimately contributes to the health, safety, and productivity of employees in the mobile car washing industry.

Personal Protective Equipment (PPE)

Personal Protective Equipment (PPE) in Mobile Car Washing Services: Ensuring Safety on the Job

In the mobile car washing service industry, the safety of employees is paramount. With the use of various cleaning chemicals, machinery, and equipment, employees are exposed to potential hazards that could lead to accidents or injuries. Personal Protective Equipment (PPE) plays a crucial role in mitigating these risks and ensuring the safety and well-being of workers on the job. By providing employees with the appropriate PPE and ensuring its proper use, mobile car washing services can create a safe working environment and prevent accidents or injuries.

One of the most common hazards faced by employees in mobile car washing services is exposure to cleaning chemicals and solutions. To protect against chemical splashes, skin irritation, or inhalation hazards, employees should wear appropriate PPE such as gloves, goggles, and respirators. Nitrile or latex gloves provide protection against contact with chemicals and solvents, while chemical-resistant goggles or safety glasses shield the eyes from splashes or fumes. Additionally, respiratory protection may be necessary when working with strong or volatile chemicals, such as using a respirator with appropriate filters to prevent inhalation of harmful vapors or gases.

Moreover, employees in mobile car washing services should wear appropriate PPE to protect against physical hazards associated with operating machinery and equipment. When using pressure washers, steam cleaners, or vacuum systems, employees should wear sturdy footwear with slip-resistant soles to prevent slips and falls. Additionally, wearing protective clothing such as coveralls or aprons can shield against cuts, abrasions, or burns from hot surfaces or moving parts. For tasks involving lifting heavy objects or working at heights, employees should use appropriate PPE such as back support belts or fall protection harnesses to prevent strains or falls.

Furthermore, employees in mobile car washing services should wear PPE to protect against environmental hazards such as extreme temperatures or weather conditions. During outdoor work in hot or sunny conditions, employees should wear hats, sunglasses, and sunscreen to protect against sunburn and heat exhaustion. In cold or rainy weather, employees should wear appropriate clothing such as jackets, gloves, and waterproof footwear to stay warm and dry. Additionally, providing employees with access to shade, hydration, and rest breaks can help prevent heat-related illnesses and ensure their comfort and well-being while working outdoors.

Health and Safety Regulations

Ensuring Health and Safety Compliance in Mobile Car Washing Services

In the mobile car washing service industry, maintaining health and safety regulations is paramount to protect both employees and customers. With the nature of the job involving the use of various cleaning chemicals, machinery, and equipment, it's crucial to adhere to strict guidelines to prevent accidents, injuries, and potential health hazards. By implementing comprehensive health and safety protocols, mobile car washing services can create a safe working environment while delivering high-quality service to their clients.

One of the primary areas of concern in mobile car washing services is the handling and use of cleaning chemicals and solutions. To comply with health and safety regulations, it's essential to properly store, handle, and dispose of cleaning chemicals in accordance with manufacturer instructions and regulatory guidelines. Ensure that employees receive adequate training on the safe use and handling of cleaning chemicals, including proper dilution ratios, personal protective equipment (PPE) requirements, and emergency procedures in case of spills or accidents.

Moreover, mobile car washing services must prioritize the safety of employees while operating machinery and equipment such as pressure washers, steam cleaners, and vacuum systems. Ensure that employees receive thorough training on the safe operation of equipment, including proper setup, usage, and shutdown procedures. Additionally, conduct regular maintenance and inspections of machinery and equipment to identify and address any issues or safety concerns promptly. Provide employees with appropriate PPE, such as gloves, goggles, and respirators, to protect against potential hazards and ensure their safety while performing tasks.

Furthermore, mobile car washing services must take measures to prevent slips, trips, and falls, both for employees and customers. Implement procedures to keep work areas clean, organized, and free of clutter, including regular sweeping, mopping, and debris removal. Additionally, use caution signs, barriers, and hazard markings to alert employees and customers to potential hazards, such as wet surfaces or uneven terrain. Provide employees with slip-resistant footwear and training on safe walking and working practices to minimize the risk of accidents and injuries.

In addition to employee safety, mobile car washing services must also consider the health and safety of customers during service delivery. Ensure that employees follow proper protocols to protect customers' vehicles and personal belongings from damage or theft while in their care. Use caution when handling customers' keys, valuables, and personal information, and implement security measures to prevent unauthorized access or misuse. Additionally, provide customers with clear instructions and safety guidelines to follow during service appointments, such as staying clear of work areas and keeping pets secured.

Moreover, mobile car washing services must comply with environmental regulations and best practices to minimize their impact on the environment. Use eco-friendly cleaning products and solutions that are biodegradable, non-toxic, and safe for use around people, pets, and plants. Additionally, implement water conservation measures, such as using low-flow pressure washers and water recycling systems, to reduce water consumption and minimize runoff. Ensure proper disposal of wastewater and cleaning chemicals in accordance with local regulations to prevent contamination of soil, waterways, and groundwater.

Furthermore, mobile car washing services must stay informed about relevant health and safety regulations, standards, and best practices to ensure ongoing compliance and continuous improvement. Stay updated on industry developments, changes in regulations, and emerging trends through industry associations, government agencies, and professional networks. Additionally, invest in ongoing training and professional development for employees to keep them informed about health and safety protocols and empower them to make informed decisions in the workplace.

In conclusion, ensuring health and safety compliance is essential for mobile car washing services to protect employees, customers, and the environment while delivering high-quality service. By implementing comprehensive health and safety protocols, including proper handling of cleaning chemicals, safe operation of equipment, prevention of slips and falls, protection of customers' vehicles and belongings, and compliance with environmental regulations, mobile car washing services can create a safe working environment and build trust and confidence among their clients. Prioritizing health and safety ultimately contributes to the success and sustainability of mobile car washing businesses in the competitive market.

Safety Measures for Employees

Safety Measures for Employees in Mobile Car Washing Services

In the bustling world of mobile car washing services, ensuring the safety of employees is paramount. With the dynamic nature of the job involving the use of various chemicals, equipment, and machinery, it's crucial to implement robust safety measures to protect employees from potential hazards and ensure a safe working environment. By prioritizing safety and adhering to best practices, mobile car washing services can minimize risks, prevent accidents, and promote the well-being of their employees.

One of the fundamental safety measures for employees in mobile car washing services is providing comprehensive training on the safe handling and use of cleaning chemicals and solutions. Employees should receive thorough instruction on the proper dilution ratios, storage procedures, and handling techniques for various cleaning products to minimize the risk of chemical exposure or injury. Additionally, employees should be trained on the appropriate use of personal protective equipment (PPE), such as gloves, goggles, and respirators, to protect against chemical splashes, inhalation hazards, and skin irritation.

Moreover, mobile car washing services must prioritize the safe operation of machinery and equipment to prevent accidents and injuries. Employees should be trained on the proper setup, usage, and maintenance of pressure washers, steam cleaners, vacuum systems, and other equipment used in car washing operations. Regular equipment inspections, maintenance checks, and repairs should be conducted to identify and address any issues or safety concerns promptly. Additionally, employees should follow manufacturer guidelines and safety protocols when operating machinery to minimize the risk of accidents or equipment failures.

Furthermore, preventing slips, trips, and falls is essential to ensure the safety of employees in mobile car washing services. Employees should keep work areas clean, organized, and free of clutter to minimize the risk of accidents. Wet or slippery surfaces should be promptly cleaned and dried, and caution signs should be used to alert employees and customers to potential hazards. Additionally, employees should wear appropriate footwear with slip-resistant soles to prevent slips and falls, especially when working outdoors or on uneven terrain.

In addition to physical safety measures, mobile car washing services must also prioritize the well-being of employees by addressing ergonomic concerns and promoting proper lifting techniques. Employees should receive training on ergonomics and body mechanics to minimize the risk of strains, sprains, and musculoskeletal injuries while performing tasks such as lifting, bending, and reaching. Additionally, providing employees with access to ergonomic tools, such as lifting aids or adjustable workstations, can help reduce the risk of injuries and promote overall comfort and well-being.

Moreover, mobile car washing services should establish clear protocols and procedures for emergency situations to ensure the safety and well-being of employees in the event of an accident or incident. Employees should be trained on emergency procedures, including evacuation routes, first aid techniques, and how to respond to fires, chemical spills, or medical emergencies. Additionally, first aid kits, fire extinguishers, and other emergency equipment should be readily accessible and regularly maintained to ensure their effectiveness in case of an emergency.

Furthermore, promoting a culture of safety and accountability among employees is essential for maintaining a safe working environment in mobile car washing services. Encourage employees to report any safety concerns, hazards, or near misses promptly so that they can be addressed and resolved. Additionally, recognize and reward employees who demonstrate a commitment to safety and adherence to safety protocols, fostering a positive safety culture within the organization.

In conclusion, safety measures for employees in mobile car washing services are essential for protecting against potential hazards and ensuring a safe working environment. By providing comprehensive training, promoting proper equipment usage and maintenance, preventing slips and falls, addressing ergonomic concerns, establishing emergency protocols, and fostering a culture of safety, mobile car washing services can prioritize the well-being of their employees and minimize the risk of accidents or injuries on the job. Ultimately, investing in employee safety contributes to the overall success and sustainability of mobile car washing businesses.

Environmental Impact and Compliance

Environmental Impact and Compliance in Mobile Car Washing Services

Mobile car washing services offer convenience and flexibility for vehicle owners, but they also come with environmental considerations that must be addressed to minimize their impact on the environment. From water conservation to chemical usage, mobile car washing services have a responsibility to operate in an environmentally responsible manner while complying with regulations and best practices. By implementing sustainable practices and ensuring compliance with environmental standards, mobile car washing services can reduce their environmental footprint and contribute to a cleaner, healthier planet.

One of the most significant environmental considerations for mobile car washing services is water usage. Traditional car washing methods can be water-intensive, leading to excessive water consumption and potential runoff pollution. To mitigate these concerns, mobile car washing services should implement water conservation measures such as using low-flow pressure washers, water recycling systems, and environmentally friendly cleaning solutions. By minimizing water usage and recycling wastewater, mobile car washing services can significantly reduce their environmental impact and conserve valuable water resources.

Moreover, mobile car washing services must be mindful of the chemicals and cleaning products they use, as these can have harmful effects on the environment if not properly managed. To minimize pollution and protect water quality, mobile car washing services should use biodegradable, non-toxic cleaning products that are safe for use around people, pets, and plants. Additionally, chemicals should be stored, handled, and disposed of according to manufacturer instructions and regulatory guidelines to prevent contamination of soil, waterways, and groundwater.

Furthermore, mobile car washing services should be aware of potential runoff pollution and take steps to prevent it during service operations. When washing vehicles outdoors, employees should avoid washing vehicles near storm drains or water bodies to prevent runoff from entering the stormwater system or natural waterways. Additionally, employees should use containment mats or barriers to capture runoff and prevent it from flowing into storm drains or sensitive areas. By implementing runoff prevention measures, mobile car washing services can protect water quality and prevent pollution of the environment.

In addition to operational considerations, mobile car washing services must ensure compliance with environmental regulations and standards to avoid fines, penalties, and legal consequences. Stay informed about relevant environmental laws, regulations, and permits applicable to mobile car washing operations at the local, state, and federal levels. Additionally, maintain records of chemical usage, water consumption, and wastewater disposal to demonstrate compliance with environmental requirements and facilitate inspections or audits by regulatory authorities.

Moreover, mobile car washing services can take proactive steps to reduce their environmental impact and promote sustainability beyond regulatory compliance. Consider implementing green initiatives such as offering eco-friendly service options, promoting waterless car washing techniques, or participating in community cleanup efforts or environmental stewardship programs. Additionally, educate customers about the environmental benefits of mobile car washing services and encourage them to choose environmentally friendly options whenever possible.

Furthermore, mobile car washing services can collaborate with suppliers, vendors, and industry partners to source sustainable materials, products, and equipment. Choose suppliers that prioritize environmental responsibility and offer eco-friendly alternatives for cleaning products, equipment, and packaging. Additionally, explore opportunities for innovation and technology adoption to improve efficiency, reduce waste, and minimize environmental impact throughout the supply chain.

In conclusion, environmental impact and compliance are significant considerations for mobile car washing services, requiring careful attention to water usage, chemical management, runoff prevention, and regulatory requirements. By implementing sustainable practices, ensuring compliance with environmental standards, and promoting environmental responsibility, mobile car washing services can minimize their environmental footprint and contribute to a cleaner, healthier planet. Ultimately, prioritizing environmental sustainability benefits not only the environment but also the long-term success and reputation of mobile car washing businesses.

Marketing Strategies for Mobile Car Wash

Effective Marketing Strategies for Mobile Car Washing Services

In the competitive world of mobile car washing services, having a robust marketing strategy is essential for attracting customers, building brand awareness, and driving business growth. From digital marketing to traditional advertising, mobile car washing services have a variety of tools and techniques at their disposal to reach potential customers and stand out in the market. By implementing creative and targeted marketing strategies, mobile car washing services can effectively promote their services and differentiate themselves from competitors.

One of the most effective marketing strategies for mobile car washing services is leveraging the power of digital marketing channels to reach a wider audience and generate leads. Establish a strong online presence by creating a professional website that showcases your services, pricing, and customer testimonials. Optimize your website for search engines (SEO) to improve visibility and attract organic traffic from potential customers searching for car washing services online. Additionally, use social media platforms such as Facebook, Instagram, and Twitter to engage with customers, share photos of your work, and run targeted advertising campaigns to reach specific demographics or geographic areas.

Moreover, consider partnering with local businesses, organizations, and events to increase brand exposure and attract new customers. Collaborate with auto dealerships, car rental agencies, or parking garages to offer discounted services or exclusive deals to their customers. Additionally, sponsor community events, fundraisers, or car shows to showcase your services and connect with potential customers in your target market. Building partnerships and participating in local events can help increase brand visibility and generate referrals from satisfied customers.

Furthermore, offering promotions, discounts, and loyalty programs is an effective way to incentivize repeat business and attract new customers to your mobile car washing service. Consider offering introductory discounts for first-time customers, referral bonuses for existing customers who refer friends or family, or loyalty rewards for frequent customers who book regular appointments. Additionally, run seasonal promotions or special offers during holidays or peak seasons to drive sales and increase customer engagement.

In addition to digital marketing and promotions, traditional advertising methods such as flyers, posters, and direct mail can still be effective for reaching local customers and generating leads for your mobile car washing service. Distribute flyers or postcards in residential neighborhoods, office complexes, or shopping centers to promote your services and attract nearby customers. Additionally, consider placing ads in local newspapers, magazines, or community newsletters to reach a broader audience and increase brand awareness.

Moreover, customer reviews and testimonials play a crucial role in influencing purchasing decisions and building trust with potential customers. Encourage satisfied customers to leave positive reviews and testimonials on your website, social media profiles, or third-party review sites such as Google My Business or Yelp. Additionally, respond promptly to customer inquiries, feedback, or complaints to demonstrate your commitment to customer satisfaction and build a positive reputation for your mobile car washing service.

Furthermore, investing in professional branding and signage can help distinguish your mobile car washing service from competitors and create a memorable impression with customers. Design a logo and brand identity that reflects your company values, personality, and commitment to quality service. Use consistent branding across all marketing materials, including website, social media profiles, business cards, and vehicle decals, to create a cohesive and recognizable brand image. Additionally, invest in high-quality signage for your mobile detailing van to attract attention and convey professionalism to potential customers.

In conclusion, implementing effective marketing strategies is essential for the success and growth of mobile car washing services. By leveraging digital marketing channels, building partnerships with local businesses, offering promotions and discounts, utilizing traditional advertising methods, collecting customer reviews and testimonials, and investing in professional branding and signage, mobile car washing services can attract customers, increase brand awareness, and differentiate themselves from competitors in the market. Ultimately, prioritizing marketing efforts helps mobile car washing services reach their target audience, drive sales, and achieve long-term success in the competitive automotive industry.

Building your Brand

Building Your Brand Identity for Mobile Car Washing Services

In the dynamic and competitive market of mobile car washing services, establishing a strong and memorable brand identity is crucial for success. Your brand is more than just a logo or a name – it's the overall perception that customers have of your business and what sets you apart from competitors. By focusing on key elements such as branding, messaging, and customer experience, mobile car washing services can create a unique and compelling brand identity that resonates with customers and drives business growth.

One of the first steps in building your brand identity for a mobile car washing service is defining your brand's values, mission, and vision. Consider what sets your business apart from competitors and what values you want to communicate to customers. Are you focused on delivering exceptional customer service, using eco-friendly cleaning products, or providing convenient and flexible service options? Clearly defining your brand's identity and values will help guide your marketing efforts and ensure consistency in messaging and customer experience.

Moreover, creating a visually appealing and cohesive brand identity is essential for capturing the attention of potential customers and building brand recognition. Develop a professional logo, color palette, and visual elements that reflect your brand's personality, values, and target audience. Use these elements consistently across all marketing materials, including your website, social media profiles, business cards, and vehicle decals, to create a cohesive and recognizable brand image.

Furthermore, crafting a compelling brand story and messaging is essential for connecting with customers on an emotional level and building brand loyalty. Share the story behind your mobile car washing service, including how you got started, what motivates you, and why you're passionate about providing exceptional service to customers. Additionally, highlight the benefits and unique selling points of your service, such as convenience, quality, or environmental sustainability, to differentiate yourself from competitors and attract customers.

In addition to branding and messaging, delivering a consistent and exceptional customer experience is key to building trust and loyalty with customers. From the first point of contact to the completion of the service, ensure that every interaction with customers reflects your brand's values and commitment to excellence. Provide clear and transparent communication, prompt responses to inquiries, and personalized service to make customers feel valued and appreciated.

Moreover, leveraging customer feedback and reviews can help strengthen your brand identity and reputation in the market. Encourage satisfied customers to leave positive reviews and testimonials on your website, social media profiles, or third-party review sites. Additionally, respond promptly and professionally to any negative feedback or complaints to demonstrate your commitment to customer satisfaction and willingness to address issues.

Furthermore, building a strong online presence through digital marketing channels is essential for reaching and engaging with potential customers in today's digital age. Establish a professional website that showcases your services, pricing, and customer testimonials, and optimize it for search engines (SEO) to improve visibility and attract organic traffic. Additionally, use social media platforms such as Facebook, Instagram, and Twitter to share photos of your work, interact with customers, and run targeted advertising campaigns to reach specific demographics or geographic areas.

In conclusion, building a strong brand identity for a mobile car washing service is essential for standing out in the competitive market and attracting customers. By defining your brand's values and mission, creating a visually appealing brand identity, crafting compelling messaging and storytelling, delivering exceptional customer experiences, leveraging customer feedback and reviews, and building a strong online presence, mobile car washing services can establish a unique and memorable brand identity that resonates with customers and drives business growth. Ultimately, prioritizing branding efforts helps mobile car washing services build trust, loyalty, and long-term success in the market.

Digital Marketing Approaches

Digital Marketing Approaches for Mobile Car Washing Services

In today's digital age, digital marketing has become an essential tool for mobile car washing services to reach and engage with potential customers effectively. By leveraging various digital channels and strategies, mobile car washing services can increase brand awareness, attract new customers, and drive business growth. From search engine optimization (SEO) to social media marketing, there are several digital marketing approaches that mobile car washing services can utilize to enhance their online presence and expand their customer base.

One of the most effective digital marketing approaches for mobile car washing services is search engine optimization (SEO). SEO involves optimizing your website and online content to rank higher in search engine results pages (SERPs) for relevant keywords and phrases. By improving your website's visibility and ranking in search engines like Google, you can attract more organic traffic and potential customers to your website. Implementing SEO best practices such as keyword research, on-page optimization, and link building can help mobile car washing services improve their search engine rankings and increase their online visibility.

Moreover, pay-per-click (PPC) advertising is another digital marketing approach that mobile car washing services can utilize to drive targeted traffic to their website and generate leads. PPC advertising involves placing ads on search engines or social media platforms and paying a fee each time a user clicks on the ad. With PPC advertising, mobile car washing services can target specific keywords, geographic locations, and demographics to reach potential customers who are actively searching for car washing services online. By carefully targeting and optimizing PPC campaigns, mobile car washing services can maximize their return on investment (ROI) and drive qualified leads to their website.

Furthermore, social media marketing is an effective digital marketing approach for mobile car washing services to engage with customers, showcase their services, and build brand awareness. Platforms such as Facebook, Instagram, and Twitter provide opportunities to share photos of your work, interact with customers, and run targeted advertising campaigns to reach specific demographics or geographic areas. By creating engaging content, responding to customer inquiries, and fostering relationships with followers, mobile car washing services can increase their visibility and attract new customers through social media marketing.

In addition to SEO, PPC advertising, and social media marketing, content marketing is another valuable digital marketing approach for mobile car washing services to establish thought leadership, provide valuable information to customers, and drive organic traffic to their website. Create informative and engaging content such as blog posts, articles, videos, and infographics that address common questions, concerns, and topics related to car washing and detailing. By publishing high-quality content regularly and optimizing it for search engines, mobile car washing services can attract organic traffic, improve their search engine rankings, and establish themselves as trusted authorities in the industry.

Moreover, email marketing is a cost-effective digital marketing approach for mobile car washing services to nurture relationships with existing customers, promote new services or specials, and drive repeat business. Build an email list of customers and prospects who have opted in to receive communications from your business, and send them regular updates, newsletters, or promotional offers. By personalizing emails based on customer preferences and behaviors, mobile car washing services can increase engagement, loyalty, and retention among their customer base.

Furthermore, online review management is an essential aspect of digital marketing for mobile car washing services to monitor and respond to customer feedback, manage their online reputation, and build trust with potential customers. Encourage satisfied customers to leave positive reviews and testimonials on your website, social media profiles, or third-party review sites such as Google My Business or Yelp. Additionally, respond promptly and professionally to any negative feedback or complaints to demonstrate your commitment to customer satisfaction and willingness to address issues.

In conclusion, digital marketing offers mobile car washing services a variety of approaches and strategies to reach and engage with potential customers online effectively. By leveraging SEO, PPC advertising, social media marketing, content marketing, email marketing, and online review management, mobile car washing services can increase brand awareness, attract new customers, and drive business growth in today's digital landscape. Ultimately, implementing a comprehensive digital marketing strategy helps mobile car washing services maximize their online presence, generate leads, and achieve long-term success in the competitive automotive industry.

Offline Marketing Tactics

Offline Marketing Tactics for Mobile Car Washing Services

While digital marketing has become increasingly popular in today's tech-savvy world, offline marketing tactics remain valuable for reaching local customers and building brand awareness for mobile car washing services. From traditional print advertising to community outreach efforts, offline marketing tactics offer unique opportunities to connect with customers in-person and establish a strong presence in the local market. By implementing creative and targeted offline marketing strategies, mobile car washing services can effectively promote their services, attract new customers, and drive business growth.

One of the most traditional offline marketing tactics for mobile car washing services is print advertising, which includes methods such as newspaper ads, flyers, brochures, and direct mail campaigns. Place advertisements in local newspapers, magazines, or community newsletters to reach a broad audience of potential customers in your target market. Additionally, distribute flyers or postcards in residential neighborhoods, office complexes, or shopping centers to promote your services and attract nearby customers. By utilizing print advertising, mobile car washing services can increase brand visibility and generate leads among local residents and businesses.

Moreover, networking and community outreach are essential offline marketing tactics for mobile car washing services to establish relationships with local businesses, organizations, and residents. Attend local networking events, business expos, or community fairs to connect with potential customers and showcase your services. Additionally, consider partnering with auto dealerships, car rental agencies, or parking garages to offer discounted services or exclusive deals to their customers. Building partnerships and participating in community events can help increase brand exposure and generate referrals from satisfied customers.

Furthermore, vehicle branding and signage are powerful offline marketing tactics for mobile car washing services to promote their services and attract attention while on the road. Invest in professional vehicle decals, wraps, or magnetic signs for your mobile detailing van to showcase your brand logo, contact information, and services. As you travel to and from customer locations, your branded vehicle acts as a mobile billboard, increasing brand visibility and awareness among potential customers in your local area.

In addition to print advertising, networking, and vehicle branding, sponsoring local events or community initiatives is another effective offline marketing tactic for mobile car washing services to build brand awareness and support the community. Sponsor community events, fundraisers, or car shows to showcase your services and connect with potential customers in your target market. Additionally, participate in local charity drives or environmental cleanup efforts to demonstrate your commitment to giving back to the community and promoting environmental stewardship.

Moreover, word-of-mouth marketing is a powerful offline marketing tactic for mobile car washing services to leverage satisfied customers as brand ambassadors and generate referrals. Encourage satisfied customers to spread the word about your services to friends, family, and colleagues by offering referral discounts or incentives. Additionally, provide exceptional service, personalized attention, and a positive customer experience to ensure that customers are happy and willing to recommend your mobile car washing service to others.

Furthermore, hosting promotional events or offering special promotions and discounts is an effective offline marketing tactic for mobile car washing services to attract new customers and drive sales. Organize a grand opening event, customer appreciation day, or seasonal promotion to offer discounted services, giveaways, or raffle prizes to attendees. Additionally, run limited-time promotions or special offers during holidays or peak seasons to incentivize customers to book appointments and try out your services. By creating excitement and offering value through promotional events and offers, mobile car washing services can attract new customers and increase brand loyalty among existing customers.

In conclusion, offline marketing tactics offer valuable opportunities for mobile car washing services to reach local customers, build brand awareness, and drive business growth. By utilizing print advertising, networking and community outreach, vehicle branding and signage, sponsoring local events, leveraging word-of-mouth marketing, and hosting promotional events, mobile car washing services can effectively promote their services, attract new customers, and establish a strong presence in the local market. Ultimately, incorporating offline marketing tactics into a comprehensive marketing strategy helps mobile car washing services maximize their reach and achieve long-term success in the competitive automotive industry.

Customer Relationship Management

Customer Relationship Management (CRM) for Mobile Car Washing Services

In the competitive market of mobile car washing services, establishing and maintaining strong relationships with customers is essential for business success and growth. Customer Relationship Management (CRM) encompasses strategies, tools, and practices aimed at managing interactions with customers throughout the customer lifecycle, from initial contact to post-service follow-up. By prioritizing CRM, mobile car washing services can enhance customer satisfaction, increase retention rates, and drive business growth.

One of the key components of effective CRM for mobile car washing services is personalized communication with customers. By collecting and maintaining comprehensive customer profiles, including contact information, service history, and preferences, mobile car washing services can tailor their communication and marketing efforts to meet the individual needs and preferences of each customer. Send personalized emails, text messages, or promotional offers based on customer preferences, service frequency, or upcoming appointments to demonstrate your attentiveness and commitment to customer satisfaction.

Moreover, proactive communication is essential for building trust and loyalty with customers in the mobile car washing industry. Keep customers informed and engaged throughout the service process by providing timely updates on appointment scheduling, service reminders, and completion notifications. Additionally, follow up with customers after service appointments to ensure satisfaction, address any concerns or issues, and gather feedback on their experience. By maintaining open lines of communication and demonstrating your dedication to customer satisfaction, mobile car washing services can build strong relationships and earn customer trust and loyalty.

Furthermore, offering exceptional customer service is crucial for maintaining positive relationships and fostering customer loyalty in the mobile car washing industry. Train your staff to deliver courteous, professional, and efficient service to every customer, regardless of the size of the job. Address customer inquiries, concerns, or complaints promptly and professionally, and take proactive steps to resolve issues and exceed customer expectations. By providing exceptional service and demonstrating your commitment to customer satisfaction, mobile car washing services can differentiate themselves from competitors and earn repeat business and referrals.

In addition to personalized communication and exceptional customer service, implementing customer loyalty programs can be an effective CRM strategy for mobile car washing services to reward repeat business and incentivize customer retention. Offer loyalty rewards such as discounts, free services, or exclusive perks to customers who book regular appointments or refer friends and family. Additionally, track customer loyalty and engagement metrics to identify opportunities for targeted marketing and promotions to reward and retain loyal customers. By recognizing and rewarding customer loyalty, mobile car washing services can strengthen relationships and encourage repeat business.

Moreover, gathering and analyzing customer feedback is essential for continuous improvement and optimization of services in the mobile car washing industry. Solicit feedback from customers through surveys, reviews, or follow-up calls to gather insights into their experience, preferences, and satisfaction levels. Use this feedback to identify areas for improvement, address customer concerns or issues, and make informed decisions to enhance the overall customer experience. Additionally, leverage customer feedback to identify trends, preferences, and opportunities for innovation and differentiation in the market.

Furthermore, utilizing CRM software and technology can streamline customer management processes and improve efficiency and effectiveness in managing customer relationships for mobile car washing services. Invest in CRM software solutions that offer features such as customer database management, appointment scheduling, communication automation, and reporting and analytics capabilities. By centralizing customer information and automating routine tasks, mobile car washing services can improve productivity, enhance communication, and deliver a seamless and personalized customer experience.

In conclusion, Customer Relationship Management (CRM) is essential for mobile car washing services to build strong, long-lasting relationships with customers and drive business growth. By prioritizing personalized communication, exceptional customer service, customer loyalty programs, feedback gathering and analysis, and leveraging CRM software and technology, mobile car washing services can enhance customer satisfaction, increase retention rates, and differentiate themselves from competitors in the market. Ultimately, investing in CRM strategies and practices helps mobile car washing services maximize customer lifetime value and achieve long-term success in the competitive automotive industry.

Customer Acquisition Strategies

Customer Acquisition Strategies for Mobile Car Washing Services

For mobile car washing services, acquiring new customers is vital for business growth and sustainability. Implementing effective customer acquisition strategies can help mobile car washing services reach their target audience, attract new customers, and increase market share. By utilizing a combination of traditional and digital marketing tactics, as well as strategic partnerships and referrals, mobile car washing services can expand their customer base and drive revenue growth.

One of the most effective customer acquisition strategies for mobile car washing services is leveraging digital marketing channels to reach potential customers online. Establish a strong online presence by creating a professional website that showcases your services, pricing, and customer testimonials. Optimize your website for search engines (SEO) to improve visibility and attract organic traffic from potential customers searching for car washing services online. Additionally, use social media platforms such as Facebook, Instagram, and Twitter to engage with customers, share photos of your work, and run targeted advertising campaigns to reach specific demographics or geographic areas.

Moreover, pay-per-click (PPC) advertising is a valuable digital marketing tactic for mobile car washing services to drive targeted traffic to their website and generate leads. With PPC advertising, mobile car washing services can place ads on search engines or social media platforms and pay a fee each time a user clicks on the ad. By carefully targeting keywords, geographic locations, and demographics, mobile car washing services can reach potential customers who are actively searching for car washing services online and drive qualified leads to their website.

Furthermore, content marketing is an effective customer acquisition strategy for mobile car washing services to establish thought leadership, provide valuable information to customers, and drive organic traffic to their website. Create informative and engaging content such as blog posts, articles, videos, and infographics that address common questions, concerns, and topics related to car washing and detailing. By publishing high-quality content regularly and optimizing it for search engines, mobile car washing services can attract organic traffic, improve their search engine rankings, and establish themselves as trusted authorities in the industry.

In addition to digital marketing tactics, traditional advertising methods such as print advertising and direct mail can still be effective for customer acquisition for mobile car washing services. Place advertisements in local newspapers, magazines, or community newsletters to reach a broad audience of potential customers in your target market. Additionally, distribute flyers or postcards in residential neighborhoods, office complexes, or shopping centers to promote your services and attract nearby customers. By utilizing traditional advertising methods, mobile car washing services can increase brand visibility and generate leads among local residents and businesses.

Moreover, strategic partnerships and referrals are valuable customer acquisition strategies for mobile car washing services to leverage existing relationships and expand their customer base. Partner with auto dealerships, car rental agencies, or parking garages to offer discounted services or exclusive deals to their customers. Additionally, incentivize satisfied customers to refer friends and family by offering referral bonuses or discounts on future services. By building partnerships and encouraging referrals, mobile car washing services can tap into new customer networks and increase brand awareness through word-of-mouth marketing.

Furthermore, participating in local events, fairs, or community initiatives is a strategic customer acquisition strategy for mobile car washing services to connect with potential customers in the local market. Sponsor community events, fundraisers, or car shows to showcase your services and engage with attendees. Additionally, host promotional events or offer special discounts and giveaways to attract new customers and generate excitement around your mobile car washing service. By participating in local events and promotions, mobile car washing services can increase brand visibility, attract new customers, and establish a presence in the community.

In conclusion, implementing effective customer acquisition strategies is essential for mobile car washing services to reach their target audience, attract new customers, and drive business growth. By leveraging digital marketing channels, traditional advertising methods, strategic partnerships and referrals, and participating in local events and promotions, mobile car washing services can expand their customer base and increase market share in the competitive automotive industry. Ultimately, prioritizing customer acquisition efforts helps mobile car washing services achieve their business goals and establish a strong foothold in the market.

Customer Retention Practices

Customer Retention Practices for Mobile Car Washing Services

In the competitive landscape of the mobile car washing industry, retaining customers is just as important as acquiring new ones. By implementing effective customer retention practices, mobile car washing services can foster loyalty, increase repeat business, and generate positive word-of-mouth referrals. From providing exceptional service to offering loyalty programs and personalized communication, there are several strategies that mobile car washing services can employ to keep customers coming back for more.

One of the most fundamental aspects of customer retention for mobile car washing services is delivering exceptional service consistently. Customers expect high-quality results and professional service when they entrust their vehicles to a mobile car washing service. Ensuring that every interaction with customers is positive, from scheduling appointments to completing the washing and detailing services, is crucial for building trust and loyalty. By consistently exceeding customer expectations and providing exceptional service, mobile car washing services can earn repeat business and positive reviews from satisfied customers.

Moreover, personalized communication is key to building strong relationships with customers and encouraging repeat business in the mobile car washing industry. Collect and maintain comprehensive customer profiles that include contact information, service history, and preferences. Use this information to personalize communication with customers, such as sending appointment reminders, follow-up emails, or special offers tailored to their preferences and service history. By demonstrating attentiveness and personalization in communication, mobile car washing services can make customers feel valued and appreciated, leading to increased loyalty and retention.

Furthermore, implementing a customer loyalty program is an effective retention strategy for mobile car washing services to reward repeat business and incentivize customer retention. Offer loyalty rewards such as discounts, free services, or exclusive perks to customers who book regular appointments or refer friends and family. Additionally, track customer loyalty and engagement metrics to identify opportunities for targeted marketing and promotions to reward and retain loyal customers. By recognizing and rewarding customer loyalty, mobile car washing services can strengthen relationships and encourage repeat business and referrals.

In addition to personalized communication and loyalty programs, gathering and acting on customer feedback is essential for customer retention in the mobile car washing industry. Solicit feedback from customers through surveys, reviews, or follow-up calls to gather insights into their experience, preferences, and satisfaction levels. Use this feedback to identify areas for improvement, address customer concerns or issues, and make informed decisions to enhance the overall customer experience. Additionally, leverage customer feedback to identify trends, preferences, and opportunities for innovation and differentiation in the market.

Moreover, maintaining a strong online reputation is critical for customer retention in the digital age. Encourage satisfied customers to leave positive reviews and testimonials on your website, social media profiles, or third-party review sites such as Google My Business or Yelp. Additionally, respond promptly and professionally to any negative feedback or complaints to demonstrate your commitment to customer satisfaction and willingness to address issues. By actively managing your online reputation and fostering positive reviews, mobile car washing services can build trust and credibility with potential customers and encourage repeat business from existing customers.

Furthermore, offering value-added services or incentives can help mobile car washing services retain customers and encourage repeat business. Consider offering additional services such as interior detailing, waxing, or upholstery cleaning to complement your core washing and detailing services. Additionally, provide special promotions or discounts for loyal customers, such as a free wash after a certain number of visits or a discounted rate for scheduling regular appointments. By offering value-added services and incentives, mobile car washing services can enhance the overall customer experience and increase customer satisfaction and retention.

In conclusion, implementing effective customer retention practices is essential for mobile car washing services to foster loyalty, increase repeat business, and generate positive word-of-mouth referrals. By providing exceptional service consistently, personalizing communication, implementing customer loyalty programs, gathering and acting on customer feedback, maintaining a strong online reputation, and offering value-added services and incentives, mobile car washing services can build strong relationships with customers and encourage long-term loyalty and retention. Ultimately, prioritizing customer retention efforts helps mobile car washing services achieve sustained success and growth in the competitive automotive industry.

Building Customer Loyalty

Building Customer Loyalty for Mobile Car Washing Services

In the realm of mobile car washing services, building customer loyalty is crucial for long-term success and sustainable growth. With numerous competitors vying for attention in the automotive industry, establishing strong relationships with customers is essential for retaining their business and fostering positive word-of-mouth referrals. By implementing effective strategies and practices, mobile car washing services can cultivate loyalty among their customer base, leading to increased repeat business and a loyal following.

One of the most fundamental aspects of building customer loyalty for mobile car washing services is delivering exceptional service consistently. Customers expect a high level of professionalism, attention to detail, and quality results when they entrust their vehicles to a mobile car washing service. Ensuring that every interaction with customers is positive, from scheduling appointments to completing the washing and detailing services, is essential for building trust and loyalty. By consistently exceeding customer expectations and providing exceptional service, mobile car washing services can earn repeat business and positive reviews from satisfied customers.

Moreover, personalized communication plays a crucial role in building customer loyalty for mobile car washing services. By collecting and maintaining comprehensive customer profiles that include contact information, service history, and preferences, mobile car washing services can personalize their communication and marketing efforts to meet the individual needs of each customer. Sending personalized emails, text messages, or promotional offers based on customer preferences, service frequency, or upcoming appointments demonstrates attentiveness and commitment to customer satisfaction, leading to increased loyalty and retention.

Furthermore, implementing a customer loyalty program is an effective strategy for mobile car washing services to reward repeat business and incentivize customer retention. Offering loyalty rewards such as discounts, free services, or exclusive perks to customers who book regular appointments or refer friends and family encourages continued engagement and loyalty. By tracking customer loyalty and engagement metrics, mobile car washing services can identify opportunities for targeted marketing and promotions to reward and retain loyal customers. Recognizing and rewarding customer loyalty helps strengthen relationships and fosters a sense of appreciation and value among customers.

In addition to personalized communication and loyalty programs, gathering and acting on customer feedback is essential for building customer loyalty in the mobile car washing industry. Soliciting feedback from customers through surveys, reviews, or follow-up calls allows mobile car washing services to gain insights into their experience, preferences, and satisfaction levels. Using this feedback to identify areas for improvement, address customer concerns or issues, and make informed decisions enhances the overall customer experience and demonstrates a commitment to customer satisfaction. Leveraging customer feedback to make positive changes and improvements fosters trust and loyalty among customers.

Moreover, maintaining a strong online reputation is critical for building customer loyalty in the digital age. Encouraging satisfied customers to leave positive reviews and testimonials on websites, social media platforms, or third-party review sites such as Google My Business or Yelp enhances credibility and trustworthiness. Responding promptly and professionally to any negative feedback or complaints demonstrates accountability and a commitment to resolving issues, further strengthening the relationship with customers. By actively managing their online reputation and fostering positive reviews, mobile car washing services can build trust and loyalty with potential customers and encourage repeat business from existing customers.

Furthermore, offering value-added services or incentives can help mobile car washing services build customer loyalty and encourage repeat business. Providing additional services such as interior detailing, waxing, or upholstery cleaning alongside core washing and detailing services enhances the overall customer experience and satisfaction. Additionally, offering special promotions or discounts for loyal customers, such as a free wash after a certain number of visits or a discounted rate for regular appointments, incentivizes continued engagement and loyalty. By offering value-added services and incentives, mobile car washing services can strengthen relationships with customers and foster long-term loyalty and retention.

In conclusion, building customer loyalty is essential for mobile car washing services to establish strong relationships with customers, increase repeat business, and generate positive word-of-mouth referrals. By delivering exceptional service consistently, personalizing communication, implementing customer loyalty programs, gathering and acting on customer feedback, maintaining a strong online reputation, and offering value-added services and incentives, mobile car washing services can cultivate loyalty among their customer base and achieve sustained success in the competitive automotive industry. Ultimately, prioritizing customer loyalty efforts helps mobile car washing services build a loyal following and foster long-term relationships with customers.

Providing Exceptional Service

Providing Exceptional Service in Mobile Car Washing

In the dynamic and competitive world of mobile car washing, delivering exceptional service is paramount for success and customer satisfaction. Whether it's a quick wash or a comprehensive detailing job, every interaction with a customer is an opportunity to showcase professionalism, quality, and dedication to excellence. By focusing on providing exceptional service, mobile car washing businesses can differentiate themselves in the market, foster customer loyalty, and drive long-term success.

One of the foundational elements of exceptional service in mobile car washing is attention to detail. Customers entrust their vehicles to mobile car washing services with the expectation of receiving a thorough and meticulous cleaning. This includes not only washing the exterior of the vehicle but also paying attention to the interior, wheels, and other hard-to-reach areas. By ensuring that every part of the vehicle receives the same level of care and attention, mobile car washing services can exceed customer expectations and leave a lasting impression.

Moreover, professionalism is key to providing exceptional service in the mobile car washing industry. From the initial point of contact to the completion of the service, every interaction with customers should be characterized by professionalism, courtesy, and respect. This includes arriving on time for appointments, maintaining a neat and organized workspace, and communicating clearly and effectively with customers. By upholding high standards of professionalism, mobile car washing services can instill confidence and trust in their customers, leading to positive experiences and repeat business.

Furthermore, using high-quality products and equipment is essential for delivering exceptional service in mobile car washing. Customers expect their vehicles to be cleaned with safe and effective cleaning solutions and state-of-the-art equipment that ensures a thorough and professional result. Investing in premium-quality cleaning products, eco-friendly solutions, and advanced washing and detailing equipment demonstrates a commitment to excellence and customer satisfaction. By using the best tools and materials available, mobile car washing services can achieve superior results and set themselves apart from competitors.

In addition to attention to detail, professionalism, and quality products, customer satisfaction should be a top priority for mobile car washing services. This means actively listening to customer needs and preferences, addressing any concerns or issues promptly and professionally, and going above and beyond to ensure a positive experience. Providing exceptional customer service, such as offering convenient scheduling options, accommodating special requests, or providing personalized recommendations, demonstrates a commitment to meeting customer needs and exceeding their expectations.

Moreover, transparency and honesty are crucial aspects of providing exceptional service in the mobile car washing industry. This includes being upfront about pricing, services offered, and any limitations or potential challenges that may arise during the cleaning process. By being transparent and honest with customers, mobile car washing services can build trust and credibility, leading to positive relationships and repeat business. Additionally, being open to feedback and willing to address customer concerns or issues demonstrates a commitment to continuous improvement and customer satisfaction.

Furthermore, ongoing training and development are essential for ensuring that mobile car washing staff are equipped with the skills, knowledge, and expertise needed to provide exceptional service. Regular training sessions on new techniques, products, and equipment help employees stay current and proficient in their roles. Additionally, providing opportunities for professional development and advancement fosters a culture of excellence and continuous improvement within the organization. By investing in the training and development of staff, mobile car washing services can ensure that every customer interaction is characterized by professionalism, expertise, and exceptional service.

In conclusion, providing exceptional service is essential for mobile car washing services to stand out in a competitive market, foster customer loyalty, and drive long-term success. By focusing on attention to detail, professionalism, quality products and equipment, customer satisfaction, transparency and honesty, and ongoing training and development, mobile car washing services can deliver exceptional service that exceeds customer expectations and leaves a lasting impression. Ultimately, prioritizing exceptional service helps mobile car washing services build positive relationships with customers and achieve sustained success in the industry.

Quality Assurance

Quality Assurance in Mobile Car Washing

In the realm of mobile car washing, ensuring quality assurance is paramount for maintaining customer satisfaction, building trust, and upholding the reputation of the business. With customers entrusting their vehicles to mobile car washing services, they expect nothing short of exceptional results and a professional experience. Quality assurance practices play a crucial role in meeting these expectations and ensuring that every service provided meets the highest standards of excellence.

One of the fundamental aspects of quality assurance in mobile car washing is the use of high-quality products and equipment. Utilizing premium-grade cleaning solutions, eco-friendly products, and state-of-the-art equipment ensures that vehicles are cleaned effectively and safely. Quality products not only contribute to superior cleaning results but also help protect the vehicle's paint, finish, and interior surfaces. By investing in quality products and equipment, mobile car washing services can deliver consistent and exceptional results to their customers.

Moreover, attention to detail is essential for maintaining quality assurance in mobile car washing. Every vehicle, regardless of its make or model, deserves thorough and meticulous attention to ensure a comprehensive cleaning. This includes not only washing the exterior of the vehicle but also addressing interior surfaces, wheels, tires, and other hard-to-reach areas. By paying attention to every detail and leaving no stone unturned, mobile car washing services can exceed customer expectations and deliver a truly exceptional service.

Furthermore, adherence to standardized processes and procedures is critical for maintaining quality assurance in mobile car washing. Establishing clear and consistent protocols for washing, detailing, and customer interactions helps ensure that every service is carried out efficiently and effectively. This includes guidelines for prepping the vehicle, selecting appropriate cleaning products, performing the wash and detailing procedures, and conducting post-service inspections. By following standardized processes, mobile car washing services can minimize errors, ensure consistency in service delivery, and maintain quality assurance across all customer interactions.

In addition to standardized processes, regular quality control inspections are essential for monitoring and maintaining service quality in mobile car washing. Conducting routine inspections of completed services allows mobile car washing services to identify any areas that may require additional attention or improvement. This includes checking for missed spots, streaks, or blemishes on the vehicle's exterior, as well as ensuring that the interior surfaces are clean and free of debris. By conducting thorough quality control inspections, mobile car washing services can address any issues promptly and ensure that every customer receives a high-quality service.

Moreover, ongoing training and development are crucial for ensuring that staff members are equipped with the skills, knowledge, and expertise needed to maintain quality assurance in mobile car washing. Providing regular training sessions on new techniques, products, and equipment helps employees stay current and proficient in their roles. Additionally, fostering a culture of continuous improvement and excellence encourages staff members to strive for excellence in every aspect of their work. By investing in the training and development of staff, mobile car washing services can ensure that quality assurance remains a top priority and that every customer receives a consistently high-quality service.

Furthermore, soliciting feedback from customers is an integral part of quality assurance in mobile car washing. Encouraging customers to provide feedback on their experience allows mobile car washing services to identify areas for improvement and address any issues or concerns promptly. This includes gathering feedback through surveys, reviews, or follow-up calls, and using this information to make informed decisions to enhance the overall customer experience. By actively seeking and acting on customer feedback, mobile car washing services can demonstrate their commitment to quality assurance and continuous improvement.

In conclusion, quality assurance is essential for maintaining customer satisfaction, building trust, and upholding the reputation of mobile car washing services. By utilizing high-quality products and equipment, paying attention to detail, adhering to standardized processes, conducting regular quality control inspections, providing ongoing training and development, and soliciting feedback from customers, mobile car washing services can ensure that every customer receives a consistently high-quality service. Ultimately, prioritizing quality assurance practices helps mobile car washing services deliver exceptional results and build long-lasting relationships with their customers.

Handling Customer Complaints

Handling Customer Complaints in Mobile Car Washing

In the mobile car washing industry, providing exceptional service is paramount for building a loyal customer base and fostering positive relationships. However, even with the best intentions and efforts, there may be occasions where customers express dissatisfaction or raise complaints about the service they have received. How a mobile car washing service handles these complaints can make a significant difference in retaining customers and preserving the reputation of the business.

The first step in effectively handling customer complaints is to listen attentively and empathetically to the customer's concerns. When a customer expresses dissatisfaction or raises a complaint, it's essential to give them your full attention and show empathy for their experience. Allow the customer to voice their concerns without interruption and demonstrate that you understand their perspective. Listening attentively to customer complaints shows that you value their feedback and are committed to addressing their concerns promptly and effectively.

Once you have listened to the customer's complaint, it's important to apologize sincerely for any inconvenience or dissatisfaction they have experienced. Regardless of the circumstances, offering a genuine apology demonstrates humility and empathy, and it helps to diffuse tension and reassure the customer that their concerns are being taken seriously. Acknowledge the customer's frustration or disappointment and express your commitment to resolving the issue to their satisfaction.

After apologizing, the next step is to investigate the complaint thoroughly to understand the root cause of the issue. Take the time to gather all relevant information, including the details of the service provided, any specific instructions given by the customer, and any factors that may have contributed to the problem. By conducting a thorough investigation, you can identify the underlying cause of the complaint and determine the best course of action to resolve it.

Once you have identified the root cause of the complaint, take proactive steps to address the issue and resolve the customer's concerns. Depending on the nature of the complaint, this may involve offering a refund or discount, providing a complimentary service to rectify the problem, or implementing changes to prevent similar issues from occurring in the future. Communicate transparently with the customer about the actions you are taking to address their concerns and ensure that they are satisfied with the resolution.

In addition to resolving the immediate issue, it's important to follow up with the customer after the complaint has been resolved to ensure their satisfaction. Reach out to the customer to confirm that the issue has been addressed to their satisfaction and to inquire if there is anything else you can do to further assist them. By following up with the customer, you demonstrate your commitment to their satisfaction and reinforce the positive relationship between the customer and your mobile car washing service.

Furthermore, use customer complaints as an opportunity to learn and improve your service delivery processes. Analyze the root causes of complaints and identify any recurring issues or trends that may require attention. Implement corrective actions or process improvements to address these issues and prevent similar complaints from arising in the future. By continuously monitoring and improving your service delivery processes, you can minimize the occurrence of customer complaints and enhance the overall customer experience.

In conclusion, handling customer complaints effectively is essential for maintaining customer satisfaction and preserving the reputation of your mobile car washing service. By listening attentively to customer concerns, apologizing sincerely, investigating complaints thoroughly, taking proactive steps to resolve issues, following up with customers after resolution, and using complaints as an opportunity to learn and improve, you can turn negative experiences into positive outcomes and build stronger relationships with your customers. Ultimately, prioritizing effective complaint handling processes helps to ensure customer satisfaction and loyalty in the competitive mobile car washing industry.

Enhancing Customer Experience

Enhancing Customer Experience in Mobile Car Washing

In the fast-paced world of mobile car washing, providing an exceptional customer experience is key to standing out in a competitive market and fostering long-term customer loyalty. From the initial point of contact to the completion of the service, every interaction with a customer is an opportunity to exceed their expectations and leave a lasting impression. By focusing on enhancing the customer experience, mobile car washing services can differentiate themselves and build strong relationships with their customers.

One of the fundamental aspects of enhancing the customer experience in mobile car washing is convenience. Mobile car washing services offer customers the convenience of having their vehicles cleaned at their preferred location, whether it's at home, at work, or elsewhere. By offering flexible scheduling options and accommodating customers' busy lifestyles, mobile car washing services can make the process of getting their vehicles cleaned as convenient and hassle-free as possible. Additionally, providing easy online booking options and streamlined appointment scheduling further enhances the convenience of the customer experience.

Moreover, personalized service is essential for enhancing the customer experience in mobile car washing. Every customer has unique preferences and expectations when it comes to their vehicle's cleaning and detailing needs. By taking the time to understand each customer's specific requirements and tailoring the service to meet their individual needs, mobile car washing services can create a personalized and memorable experience for their customers. Whether it's using a particular cleaning product, addressing specific areas of concern, or accommodating special requests, personalized service demonstrates attentiveness and a commitment to customer satisfaction.

Furthermore, communication plays a crucial role in enhancing the customer experience in mobile car washing. Clear and timely communication with customers, from scheduling appointments to providing updates on the service progress, helps to build trust and confidence in the service provided. Keep customers informed about their appointment status, arrival times, and any delays or changes to the schedule to ensure a smooth and stress-free experience. Additionally, proactively reaching out to customers after the service to gather feedback and address any concerns further demonstrates a commitment to communication and customer satisfaction.

In addition to convenience, personalized service, and communication, delivering exceptional results is paramount for enhancing the customer experience in mobile car washing. Customers expect their vehicles to be cleaned thoroughly and professionally, with attention to detail and a high level of quality. Utilizing premium-grade cleaning products, eco-friendly solutions, and state-of-the-art equipment ensures that vehicles are cleaned effectively and safely, leaving them looking immaculate both inside and out. By consistently delivering exceptional results, mobile car washing services can exceed customer expectations and leave a positive lasting impression.

Moreover, going the extra mile to add value to the customer experience can make a significant difference in building loyalty and satisfaction. Offering additional services such as interior detailing, waxing, or upholstery cleaning alongside core washing and detailing services enhances the overall customer experience and satisfaction. Additionally, providing complimentary services, special promotions, or loyalty rewards for repeat customers demonstrates appreciation and fosters a sense of loyalty and goodwill.

Furthermore, actively seeking and acting on customer feedback is essential for continuously improving and enhancing the customer experience in mobile car washing. Encourage customers to provide feedback on their experience, whether it's through surveys, reviews, or follow-up calls, and use this information to identify areas for improvement and make informed decisions to enhance the overall customer experience. By listening to customer feedback and implementing changes based on their suggestions, mobile car washing services can demonstrate their commitment to customer satisfaction and continuous improvement.

In conclusion, enhancing the customer experience is essential for mobile car washing services to differentiate themselves, build strong relationships with customers, and foster long-term loyalty and satisfaction. By focusing on convenience, personalized service, communication, delivering exceptional results, adding value to the customer experience, and actively seeking customer feedback, mobile car washing services can create memorable and positive experiences for their customers. Ultimately, prioritizing the customer experience helps mobile car washing services stand out in a competitive market and achieve sustained success and growth.

Incorporating Technology into Operations

Incorporating Technology into Mobile Car Washing Operations

In the ever-evolving landscape of mobile car washing, staying ahead of the curve means embracing technological advancements to streamline operations, enhance efficiency, and improve the overall customer experience. With the advent of innovative technologies, mobile car washing services now have access to a wide array of tools and solutions that can revolutionize how they operate and deliver services to their customers. By incorporating technology into their operations, mobile car washing services can optimize their workflows, increase productivity, and stay competitive in the market.

One of the primary ways mobile car washing services can incorporate technology into their operations is through the use of mobile apps and software solutions. Mobile apps designed specifically for car washing businesses offer a range of features and functionalities, including appointment scheduling, customer management, route optimization, and payment processing. These apps streamline administrative tasks, allowing mobile car washing services to manage appointments, track customer information, and process payments more efficiently. Additionally, mobile apps can provide real-time updates and notifications to customers, keeping them informed about their appointments and service status.

Moreover, leveraging GPS and mapping technology can significantly improve the efficiency of mobile car washing operations. Route optimization software allows mobile car washing services to plan and optimize their service routes based on factors such as location, traffic conditions, and appointment schedules. By optimizing routes, mobile car washing services can minimize travel time, reduce fuel costs, and maximize the number of appointments completed in a day. This not only improves operational efficiency but also enhances the overall customer experience by ensuring timely and punctual service delivery.

Furthermore, the integration of mobile payment solutions into mobile car washing operations can streamline the payment process and improve customer convenience. Mobile payment platforms allow customers to pay for services securely and conveniently using their smartphones or other mobile devices. By offering mobile payment options, mobile car washing services can eliminate the need for cash transactions, reduce administrative overhead, and provide customers with a seamless and hassle-free payment experience. Additionally, mobile payment solutions can help mobile car washing services attract new customers and differentiate themselves in the market by offering modern and convenient payment options.

In addition to mobile apps, route optimization software, and mobile payment solutions, leveraging automation technology can further enhance efficiency and productivity in mobile car washing operations. Automated systems for tasks such as appointment scheduling, customer notifications, and service reminders can help mobile car washing services streamline their workflows and reduce manual intervention. For example, automated appointment reminders can help reduce no-shows and cancellations by sending customers reminders about their upcoming appointments via email or SMS. Similarly, automated service reminders can prompt customers to schedule their next appointment when their vehicle is due for another wash or detailing service.

Moreover, implementing customer relationship management (CRM) software can help mobile car washing services manage and nurture customer relationships more effectively. CRM software allows mobile car washing services to track customer interactions, manage customer information, and personalize communication with customers. By centralizing customer data and communication channels, CRM software enables mobile car washing services to deliver more personalized and targeted marketing campaigns, follow up with customers after service appointments, and provide a higher level of customer service.

In conclusion, incorporating technology into mobile car washing operations is essential for staying competitive, improving efficiency, and enhancing the overall customer experience. By leveraging mobile apps, route optimization software, mobile payment solutions, automation technology, and CRM software, mobile car washing services can streamline their workflows, increase productivity, and provide customers with modern and convenient service options. Ultimately, embracing technology enables mobile car washing services to stay ahead of the curve and deliver exceptional service in an increasingly digital world.

Using Business Software

In the fast-paced and competitive world of mobile car washing, managing operations efficiently is crucial for success. One of the most effective ways to streamline processes, enhance productivity, and improve overall business performance is by utilizing business software tailored to the unique needs of mobile car washing services. From scheduling appointments to managing customer relationships, business software offers a wide range of tools and functionalities designed to optimize workflows and drive success.

One of the key benefits of using business software in mobile car washing operations is improved organization and scheduling. Business software allows mobile car washing services to efficiently manage appointments, allocate resources, and optimize service routes. By centralizing appointment scheduling and customer information in a single platform, business software helps eliminate scheduling conflicts, minimize downtime, and ensure that every customer receives timely and punctual service. Additionally, advanced scheduling features such as route optimization help mobile car washing services maximize efficiency by planning the most efficient service routes based on factors such as location, traffic conditions, and appointment priorities.

Moreover, business software enables mobile car washing services to better manage customer relationships and enhance communication. Customer relationship management (CRM) software allows mobile car washing services to centralize customer information, track interactions, and personalize communication with customers. By maintaining a comprehensive database of customer information, including service history, preferences, and contact details, mobile car washing services can deliver more personalized and targeted marketing campaigns, follow up with customers after service appointments, and provide a higher level of customer service. Additionally, CRM software facilitates communication with customers through automated reminders, notifications, and personalized messages, helping to strengthen relationships and improve customer satisfaction.

Furthermore, business software offers powerful tools for managing finances and tracking business performance. Accounting software allows mobile car washing services to streamline financial processes, track income and expenses, and generate detailed financial reports. By automating tasks such as invoicing, payment processing, and expense tracking, accounting software helps mobile car washing services save time, reduce errors, and maintain accurate financial records. Additionally, advanced reporting features provide valuable insights into business performance, allowing mobile car washing services to identify trends, track key performance indicators, and make data-driven decisions to drive growth and profitability.

In addition to organization, scheduling, customer relationship management, and financial management, business software offers a wide range of other features and functionalities designed to optimize various aspects of mobile car washing operations. Inventory management software helps mobile car washing services track and manage supplies, equipment, and inventory levels, ensuring that they have the necessary resources to fulfill customer orders efficiently. Workflow automation tools streamline repetitive tasks and processes, freeing up time for employees to focus on more strategic activities. Additionally, analytics and reporting tools provide valuable insights into business performance, allowing mobile car washing services to identify opportunities for improvement and make informed decisions to drive growth and success.

In conclusion, using business software is essential for mobile car washing services to streamline operations, enhance productivity, and drive success. From scheduling appointments to managing customer relationships, tracking finances, and optimizing workflows, business software offers a wide range of tools and functionalities designed to meet the unique needs of mobile car washing operations. By leveraging business software, mobile car washing services can improve organization, enhance communication, manage finances, and optimize various aspects of their operations, ultimately driving growth, profitability, and customer satisfaction.

Mobile Apps for Efficiency

Mobile Apps for Enhanced Efficiency in Mobile Car Washing

In today's fast-paced world, mobile car washing services are continually seeking innovative ways to enhance efficiency, improve service delivery, and exceed customer expectations. One such solution that has gained significant traction in recent years is the use of mobile apps tailored specifically for mobile car washing businesses. These apps offer a wide range of features and functionalities designed to streamline operations, optimize workflows, and enhance the overall customer experience. From appointment scheduling to route optimization and payment processing, mobile apps have revolutionized the way mobile car washing services operate, leading to increased efficiency and productivity across the board.

One of the primary benefits of using mobile apps in mobile car washing operations is improved appointment scheduling and management. Mobile apps allow customers to book appointments conveniently from their smartphones or tablets, eliminating the need for phone calls or emails. By offering a user-friendly interface and real-time availability, mobile apps make it easy for customers to schedule appointments at their preferred time and location, whether it's at home, at work, or elsewhere. This not only saves time for both customers and service providers but also helps reduce scheduling conflicts and minimize downtime, leading to more efficient use of resources and increased customer satisfaction.

Moreover, mobile apps enable mobile car washing services to optimize service routes and maximize efficiency. Advanced route optimization algorithms analyze factors such as location, traffic conditions, and appointment priorities to plan the most efficient service routes for mobile car washing vehicles. By optimizing routes, mobile apps help minimize travel time, reduce fuel costs, and maximize the number of appointments completed in a day. This not only improves operational efficiency but also enhances the overall customer experience by ensuring timely and punctual service delivery.

Furthermore, mobile apps facilitate seamless communication and collaboration between mobile car washing service providers and their customers. Built-in messaging features allow customers to communicate directly with service providers, ask questions, and provide feedback in real-time. Additionally, push notifications keep customers informed about appointment status, service updates, and promotional offers, helping to enhance engagement and retention. By fostering open and transparent communication, mobile apps help build trust and confidence in the service provided, leading to stronger customer relationships and increased loyalty over time.

In addition to appointment scheduling, route optimization, and communication, mobile apps offer a wide range of other features and functionalities designed to enhance efficiency in mobile car washing operations. For example, mobile apps can integrate with payment processing systems to enable secure and convenient mobile payments. By allowing customers to pay for services directly through the app using their preferred payment method, mobile apps help streamline the payment process and reduce administrative overhead for mobile car washing services. Additionally, mobile apps can provide access to customer information, service history, and appointment details, allowing service providers to deliver more personalized and tailored service to each customer.

Moreover, mobile apps offer valuable analytics and reporting tools that provide insights into business performance and customer behavior. By tracking key metrics such as appointment volume, revenue, customer satisfaction scores, and service completion rates, mobile apps help mobile car washing services identify areas for improvement and make informed decisions to drive growth and success. Additionally, advanced reporting features allow service providers to generate custom reports, analyze trends, and track progress towards business goals, helping to optimize operations and maximize profitability over time.

In conclusion, mobile apps have become indispensable tools for enhancing efficiency in mobile car washing operations. By offering features such as appointment scheduling, route optimization, communication, payment processing, and analytics, mobile apps streamline workflows, improve service delivery, and drive success for mobile car washing businesses. As the demand for mobile car washing services continues to grow, leveraging mobile apps is essential for staying competitive, meeting customer expectations, and achieving long-term success in the industry.

Customer Payment Options

Customer Payment Options in Mobile Car Washing Services

In the dynamic world of mobile car washing services, offering convenient and flexible payment options is crucial for enhancing the overall customer experience and driving satisfaction. With advancements in technology and changing consumer preferences, mobile car washing services have expanded their payment options beyond traditional methods to accommodate a diverse range of customer preferences and needs. By providing multiple payment options, mobile car washing services can streamline the payment process, improve customer convenience, and build stronger relationships with their clientele.

One of the most common payment options offered by mobile car washing services is cash payment. Cash payments provide customers with a straightforward and familiar way to pay for services rendered. Many customers prefer cash payments due to their simplicity and immediacy, as they allow customers to complete the transaction quickly and without the need for additional steps. Additionally, cash payments offer a sense of security and control for customers who prefer to pay with physical currency. Mobile car washing services that accept cash payments typically collect payment from customers directly at the time of service, either before or after the car washing and detailing process.

Another popular payment option for mobile car washing services is credit and debit card payments. With the widespread adoption of electronic payment technology, many customers prefer to pay for services using their credit or debit cards. Mobile car washing services that accept card payments typically use mobile card readers or point-of-sale (POS) systems to process transactions securely and efficiently. Accepting card payments offers several benefits for both customers and service providers, including increased convenience, faster transaction processing times, and enhanced security. Additionally, card payments allow customers to track their expenses more easily and provide a digital record of their transactions for future reference.

Furthermore, mobile car washing services can offer digital payment options such as mobile wallets and online payment platforms. Mobile wallets, such as Apple Pay, Google Pay, and Samsung Pay, allow customers to store their payment information securely on their smartphones and make contactless payments at the point of service. Similarly, online payment platforms such as PayPal, Venmo, and Square Cash enable customers to pay for services online using their preferred payment method. Digital payment options offer convenience and flexibility for customers, allowing them to make payments anytime, anywhere, without the need for cash or physical cards.

Additionally, mobile car washing services can offer subscription-based payment models for customers who require regular and recurring car washing services. Subscription-based payment models allow customers to sign up for a monthly or quarterly subscription plan and receive a predetermined number of car washes or detailing services each billing cycle. By offering subscription-based payment options, mobile car washing services can provide customers with a convenient and hassle-free way to maintain the cleanliness and appearance of their vehicles on a regular basis. Subscription plans also help mobile car washing services generate recurring revenue and build long-term customer relationships.

Moreover, mobile car washing services can explore alternative payment methods such as contactless payments and cryptocurrency payments to cater to the evolving needs and preferences of their customers. Contactless payments, which use near-field communication (NFC) technology to enable tap-and-go transactions, offer a convenient and hygienic way for customers to pay for services without physical contact. Similarly, accepting cryptocurrency payments such as Bitcoin and Ethereum can appeal to tech-savvy customers who prefer decentralized digital currencies. By offering a diverse range of payment options, mobile car washing services can cater to the diverse needs and preferences of their customer base, enhance the overall customer experience, and drive satisfaction and loyalty over time.

Managing and Leading Your Business

Managing and Leading Your Mobile Car Washing Business

Running a successful mobile car washing business requires not only effective management of day-to-day operations but also strong leadership to guide the business towards growth and success. As the owner or manager of a mobile car washing service, it is essential to wear multiple hats, balancing operational responsibilities with strategic decision-making and leadership. By adopting effective management and leadership practices, mobile car washing businesses can optimize their operations, foster a positive work environment, and achieve their business goals.

One of the key aspects of managing a mobile car washing business is efficient resource management. This includes managing human resources, equipment, supplies, and finances to ensure optimal efficiency and productivity. Effective scheduling and resource allocation help mobile car washing businesses maximize their capacity and serve as many customers as possible while minimizing downtime and waste. By carefully managing resources, mobile car washing businesses can optimize their operations, reduce costs, and improve overall profitability.

Furthermore, effective communication is essential for managing a mobile car washing business successfully. Clear and transparent communication with employees, customers, and other stakeholders helps ensure that everyone is on the same page and working towards common goals. Providing regular updates, setting clear expectations, and soliciting feedback from employees and customers foster a culture of open communication and collaboration, which is crucial for the success of any business. Additionally, effective communication helps resolve conflicts, address issues, and build trust and loyalty among employees and customers.

Moreover, effective leadership is essential for guiding a mobile car washing business towards growth and success. A strong leader sets the vision and direction for the business, inspires and motivates employees, and leads by example. Effective leaders empower employees to take ownership of their roles and responsibilities, foster a positive work culture, and create a sense of camaraderie and teamwork among employees. By providing guidance, support, and mentorship, effective leaders help employees develop their skills, achieve their full potential, and contribute to the overall success of the business.

In addition to managing day-to-day operations and providing leadership, effective business leaders also focus on strategic planning and decision-making. This involves setting clear goals and objectives for the business, identifying growth opportunities, and developing strategies to achieve long-term success. By analyzing market trends, assessing competition, and staying abreast of industry developments, business leaders can make informed decisions and steer the business in the right direction. Additionally, effective leaders are proactive in identifying challenges and opportunities, adapting to changes in the market, and positioning the business for growth and sustainability.

Furthermore, effective leaders prioritize customer satisfaction and quality service delivery in their mobile car washing businesses. By focusing on providing exceptional service and exceeding customer expectations, mobile car washing businesses can build a loyal customer base and differentiate themselves from competitors. Effective leaders emphasize the importance of quality, professionalism, and attention to detail in every aspect of the business, from customer interactions to service delivery. By instilling a customer-centric mindset among employees and consistently delivering high-quality service, mobile car washing businesses can earn the trust and loyalty of their customers and drive repeat business and referrals.

In conclusion, managing and leading a mobile car washing business requires a combination of effective management practices and strong leadership skills. By efficiently managing resources, communicating effectively, providing strong leadership, and focusing on strategic planning and decision-making, mobile car washing businesses can optimize their operations, foster a positive work environment, and achieve long-term success. Effective management and leadership are essential for guiding mobile car washing businesses towards growth, profitability, and sustainability in an increasingly competitive market.

Role of a Business Owner

The Role of a Business Owner in Running a Mobile Car Washing Service

In the dynamic and competitive industry of mobile car washing services, the role of the business owner is multifaceted and essential for the success and growth of the business. As the driving force behind the operation, the business owner plays a pivotal role in setting the vision, strategy, and direction of the mobile car washing service. From managing day-to-day operations to making strategic decisions and leading the team, the business owner's responsibilities are diverse and impactful.

One of the primary responsibilities of a business owner in the mobile car washing industry is setting the vision and strategic direction for the business. The business owner defines the mission, goals, and objectives of the mobile car washing service and develops a roadmap for achieving them. By analyzing market trends, identifying opportunities, and assessing competitive threats, the business owner can develop a clear vision for the business and align the team's efforts towards its realization.

Moreover, the business owner is responsible for developing and implementing effective business strategies to drive growth and profitability. This involves identifying target markets, developing marketing strategies, and establishing pricing and service offerings that resonate with customers. Additionally, the business owner oversees financial management, including budgeting, forecasting, and monitoring financial performance, to ensure the business remains viable and sustainable in the long term.

Furthermore, the business owner plays a crucial role in managing and leading the team of employees in the mobile car washing service. This includes hiring and training employees, setting performance expectations, and providing ongoing support and feedback to ensure the team performs at its best. Effective leadership is essential for fostering a positive work culture, motivating employees, and creating a cohesive and productive team environment.

In addition to managing the team, the business owner is responsible for ensuring the quality of service delivery and customer satisfaction. By setting high standards for service quality, professionalism, and customer care, the business owner helps differentiate the mobile car washing service from competitors and build a loyal customer base. Additionally, the business owner solicits feedback from customers and uses it to continuously improve service offerings and enhance the overall customer experience.

Moreover, the business owner is tasked with overseeing operational efficiency and effectiveness in the mobile car washing service. This involves optimizing workflows, streamlining processes, and leveraging technology to maximize productivity and minimize costs. By investing in tools and equipment, implementing efficient scheduling and routing systems, and adopting best practices in operations management, the business owner can improve efficiency and profitability in the mobile car washing service.

Furthermore, the business owner is responsible for staying abreast of industry trends, regulations, and developments that may impact the mobile car washing service. This involves attending industry conferences, networking with other professionals, and staying informed about changes in consumer preferences, environmental regulations, and technological advancements. By staying ahead of the curve, the business owner can position the mobile car washing service for success and capitalize on emerging opportunities in the market.

In conclusion, the role of a business owner in running a mobile car washing service is diverse and multifaceted. From setting the vision and strategic direction to managing day-to-day operations, leading the team, and ensuring customer satisfaction, the business owner's responsibilities are integral to the success and growth of the business. By effectively managing resources, driving innovation, and fostering a culture of excellence, the business owner can position the mobile car washing service for long-term success and profitability in the competitive marketplace.

Leadership Strategies

In the realm of mobile car washing services, effective leadership is paramount to navigating the complexities of the industry, managing teams, and steering the business towards success. Leadership strategies tailored to the unique demands of mobile car washing services can empower business owners to inspire their teams, drive innovation, and cultivate a culture of excellence. By implementing the right leadership strategies, mobile car washing service owners can foster employee engagement, enhance customer satisfaction, and achieve sustainable growth.

One key leadership strategy for mobile car washing service owners is leading by example. Business owners who lead by example set a standard of excellence for their teams and inspire them to strive for greatness. Whether it's demonstrating meticulous attention to detail during a car washing service or going the extra mile to ensure customer satisfaction, leading by example instills a sense of pride and dedication among employees. By embodying the values and principles of the business, business owners can earn the respect and trust of their teams and motivate them to deliver their best work.

Another essential leadership strategy for mobile car washing service owners is effective communication. Clear and transparent communication is critical for aligning team members' goals and expectations, fostering collaboration, and driving business success. Business owners should communicate openly with their teams, providing regular updates, sharing company goals and objectives, and soliciting feedback and ideas from employees. By fostering a culture of open communication, business owners can empower their teams to share their thoughts and concerns, identify opportunities for improvement, and contribute to the overall success of the business.

Moreover, effective delegation is a crucial leadership strategy for mobile car washing service owners. Delegating tasks and responsibilities allows business owners to leverage the skills and expertise of their team members, distribute workload more effectively, and focus on strategic priorities. Business owners should delegate tasks based on team members' strengths, capabilities, and development goals, providing clear instructions and support as needed. By empowering employees to take ownership of their roles and responsibilities, business owners can foster a sense of accountability, autonomy, and empowerment among their teams.

Additionally, fostering a culture of continuous learning and development is essential for effective leadership in mobile car washing services. Business owners should invest in training and development programs to help employees enhance their skills, expand their knowledge, and stay abreast of industry trends and best practices. By providing opportunities for growth and advancement, business owners can inspire loyalty and commitment among their teams and cultivate a culture of continuous improvement and innovation.

Furthermore, effective leadership in mobile car washing services requires a focus on customer-centricity. Business owners should prioritize customer satisfaction and service excellence, instilling a customer-first mindset among their teams. By emphasizing the importance of professionalism, courtesy, and quality in every customer interaction, business owners can build strong relationships with their clientele and differentiate their mobile car washing service from competitors. Additionally, business owners should actively seek feedback from customers, listen to their concerns, and take proactive steps to address any issues or opportunities for improvement.

In conclusion, effective leadership is essential for success in the mobile car washing industry. By implementing leadership strategies such as leading by example, effective communication, delegation, continuous learning and development, and customer-centricity, business owners can inspire their teams, drive innovation, and achieve sustainable growth. By fostering a culture of excellence, empowerment, and customer satisfaction, business owners can position their mobile car washing services for long-term success and profitability in the competitive marketplace.

Team Building and Communication Skills

In the dynamic and fast-paced environment of mobile car washing services, effective team building and communication skills are essential for success. Mobile car washing businesses rely heavily on cohesive teams that can efficiently work together to deliver exceptional service to customers. By fostering strong team dynamics and promoting open communication, mobile car washing service owners can enhance productivity, boost morale, and achieve greater customer satisfaction.

Team building is a critical aspect of running a successful mobile car washing service. Building a strong team starts with recruiting individuals who are not only skilled and experienced but also share the company's values and vision. Mobile car washing service owners should prioritize hiring team members who demonstrate reliability, professionalism, and a strong work ethic. Additionally, diversity in skill sets and backgrounds can bring fresh perspectives and ideas to the team, contributing to innovation and problem-solving.

Once the team is assembled, mobile car washing service owners can implement various team-building activities and initiatives to foster camaraderie and collaboration. Team-building activities such as group outings, team-building exercises, and team-building workshops can help break down barriers, build trust, and strengthen relationships among team members. Moreover, team-building initiatives should be ongoing, with regular opportunities for team members to bond, celebrate successes, and support one another.

Effective communication is another cornerstone of successful team building in mobile car washing services. Clear and transparent communication is essential for ensuring that team members understand their roles and responsibilities, goals and objectives, and expectations for performance. Mobile car washing service owners should establish open channels of communication, providing regular updates, feedback, and guidance to their teams. Additionally, fostering a culture of open communication encourages team members to share ideas, concerns, and feedback, contributing to continuous improvement and innovation within the business.

Moreover, mobile car washing service owners should invest in communication training and development for their teams. Effective communication skills, such as active listening, empathy, and conflict resolution, are essential for building strong relationships and resolving issues effectively. By providing communication training and development opportunities, mobile car washing service owners can equip their teams with the skills and tools they need to communicate effectively with customers and colleagues alike.

In addition to verbal communication, nonverbal communication skills are also crucial in the mobile car washing industry. Team members must be able to convey professionalism, courtesy, and confidence through their body language, facial expressions, and demeanor. Mobile car washing service owners should train their teams to project a positive and approachable image, both in person and when interacting with customers remotely.

Furthermore, mobile car washing service owners should leverage technology to facilitate communication and collaboration among team members. Mobile apps, messaging platforms, and project management tools can help streamline communication, coordinate schedules, and share important information in real-time. Additionally, video conferencing tools can facilitate virtual meetings and training sessions, allowing team members to connect and collaborate regardless of their location.

In conclusion, effective team building and communication skills are essential for success in the mobile car washing industry. By fostering strong team dynamics, promoting open communication, and leveraging technology, mobile car washing service owners can create cohesive and productive teams that deliver exceptional service to customers. Investing in team building and communication skills not only enhances productivity and efficiency but also fosters a positive work culture and drives long-term success in the competitive marketplace.

Analysing Business Performance

Analyzing Business Performance in the Mobile Car Washing Industry

In the fast-paced and competitive world of mobile car washing services, analyzing business performance is crucial for identifying strengths, weaknesses, opportunities, and threats. By carefully evaluating key performance indicators (KPIs) and metrics, mobile car washing service owners can gain valuable insights into their business operations, make informed decisions, and drive continuous improvement and growth. From financial performance to customer satisfaction and operational efficiency, analyzing business performance enables mobile car washing service owners to optimize their operations and achieve their business goals.

Financial performance is one of the primary areas of focus when analyzing business performance in the mobile car washing industry. Mobile car washing service owners should regularly review financial statements, such as income statements, balance sheets, and cash flow statements, to assess the overall financial health of the business. By tracking revenue, expenses, and profitability metrics, business owners can identify areas of opportunity for cost savings, revenue growth, and improved profitability. Additionally, financial analysis enables business owners to monitor cash flow, manage working capital effectively, and make strategic financial decisions to support business growth and sustainability.

Moreover, customer satisfaction is a critical aspect of business performance in the mobile car washing industry. Analyzing customer feedback, reviews, and satisfaction surveys provides valuable insights into the quality of service delivery and customer experience. Mobile car washing service owners should track metrics such as customer satisfaction scores, net promoter scores (NPS), and customer retention rates to gauge customer loyalty and identify areas for improvement. By addressing customer concerns and continuously striving to exceed customer expectations, business owners can enhance customer satisfaction, drive repeat business, and build a loyal customer base.

Operational efficiency is another key area of focus when analyzing business performance in the mobile car washing industry. Business owners should assess operational metrics such as service throughput, vehicle turnaround time, and resource utilization to identify inefficiencies and bottlenecks in the service delivery process. By streamlining workflows, optimizing scheduling and routing, and leveraging technology solutions, mobile car washing service owners can improve operational efficiency, reduce costs, and enhance overall productivity. Additionally, operational analysis enables business owners to identify opportunities for process improvement and innovation to stay competitive in the market.

Furthermore, analyzing marketing and sales performance is essential for driving customer acquisition and revenue growth in the mobile car washing industry. Business owners should track metrics such as customer acquisition cost (CAC), conversion rates, and return on investment (ROI) for marketing campaigns to assess the effectiveness of their marketing efforts. By analyzing marketing and sales data, business owners can identify the most successful marketing channels, target customer segments, and promotional strategies to optimize marketing spend and drive sales growth.

In addition to financial, customer, operational, and marketing performance, business owners should also consider regulatory compliance and environmental sustainability when analyzing business performance in the mobile car washing industry. Compliance with local regulations and environmental standards is essential for maintaining the reputation and integrity of the business. Business owners should track metrics related to regulatory compliance, environmental impact, and sustainability initiatives to ensure adherence to legal requirements and demonstrate corporate responsibility.

In conclusion, analyzing business performance is essential for driving success and growth in the mobile car washing industry. By evaluating key performance indicators across financial, customer, operational, marketing, regulatory, and environmental dimensions, business owners can gain valuable insights into their business operations and make informed decisions to optimize performance and achieve their business goals. Continuous monitoring, analysis, and improvement are essential for staying competitive and driving long-term success in the dynamic and evolving mobile car washing market.

Understanding Financial Statements

Understanding Financial Statements in the Context of a Mobile Car Washing Service

Financial statements are vital tools that provide valuable insights into the financial health and performance of a business, including mobile car washing services. These statements offer a snapshot of the company's financial position, performance, and cash flow, allowing business owners to make informed decisions, track progress, and plan for the future.

One of the primary financial statements that business owners in the mobile car washing industry rely on is the income statement, also known as the profit and loss statement. This statement summarizes the revenues, expenses, and net income of the business over a specific period, typically monthly, quarterly, or annually. For a mobile car washing service, revenue sources may include fees charged for car washes, detailing services, and additional add-ons such as waxing or interior cleaning. On the other hand, expenses may include labor costs, equipment maintenance, supplies, fuel, and marketing expenses. By analyzing the income statement, business owners can assess their profitability, identify areas of cost inefficiency, and make adjustments to improve financial performance.

Another crucial financial statement for mobile car washing services is the balance sheet. The balance sheet provides a snapshot of the company's financial position at a specific point in time, detailing its assets, liabilities, and equity. Assets typically include cash, equipment, vehicles, and accounts receivable, while liabilities may consist of accounts payable, loans, and other debts. Equity represents the difference between assets and liabilities and reflects the owner's investment in the business. By analyzing the balance sheet, business owners can assess their liquidity, solvency, and overall financial stability, which is crucial for making strategic decisions and securing financing for growth and expansion.

Furthermore, the cash flow statement is essential for understanding how cash moves in and out of the business over a specific period. This statement categorizes cash inflows and outflows into operating, investing, and financing activities. For a mobile car washing service, cash inflows may include revenue from car wash services, while cash outflows may include expenses such as payroll, equipment purchases, and loan repayments. By analyzing the cash flow statement, business owners can evaluate their ability to generate cash, manage liquidity, and fund ongoing operations and investments.

In addition to the primary financial statements, business owners in the mobile car washing industry may also utilize other financial reports and metrics to assess performance and track progress. For example, key performance indicators (KPIs) such as average revenue per car wash, customer acquisition cost, and customer retention rate provide valuable insights into business performance and efficiency. Trend analysis, ratio analysis, and benchmarking against industry standards can also help business owners identify areas of strength and weakness and make informed decisions to drive growth and profitability.

Moreover, understanding financial statements is not only essential for business owners but also for stakeholders such as investors, lenders, and potential partners. Accurate and transparent financial reporting instills confidence in stakeholders and demonstrates the business's credibility and financial health. Therefore, business owners should ensure that their financial statements are prepared accurately and in accordance with generally accepted accounting principles (GAAP) to maintain transparency and integrity.

In conclusion, understanding financial statements is essential for business owners in the mobile car washing industry to assess performance, make informed decisions, and drive growth and profitability. By analyzing income statements, balance sheets, cash flow statements, and other financial reports, business owners can gain valuable insights into their financial position, performance, and cash flow, enabling them to plan effectively and achieve their business goals.

Key Performance Indicators (KPI)

Key Performance Indicators (KPIs) are essential metrics that help mobile car washing service owners measure their business's performance, track progress, and identify areas for improvement. By monitoring KPIs regularly, business owners can make informed decisions, optimize operations, and drive growth and profitability in the competitive mobile car washing industry.

One crucial KPI for mobile car washing services is customer satisfaction. Customer satisfaction measures the level of satisfaction and happiness among customers with the service provided by the mobile car washing business. This KPI can be assessed through customer feedback, surveys, and reviews, as well as metrics such as Net Promoter Score (NPS) and customer retention rate. High levels of customer satisfaction indicate that the business is meeting or exceeding customer expectations, fostering loyalty, and driving repeat business.

Another important KPI for mobile car washing services is service throughput or the number of cars serviced within a specific period. Service throughput measures the efficiency and productivity of the mobile car washing operation and helps business owners assess their capacity to meet customer demand. By tracking service throughput, business owners can identify bottlenecks, optimize scheduling and routing, and improve operational efficiency to maximize revenue and profitability.

Furthermore, average revenue per car wash is a key financial KPI for mobile car washing services. This metric measures the average revenue generated from each car wash service provided by the business. By calculating average revenue per car wash, business owners can assess pricing strategies, upselling effectiveness, and overall revenue generation. Increasing average revenue per car wash through add-on services or premium packages can help boost profitability and revenue growth.

Additionally, customer acquisition cost (CAC) is an important KPI for mobile car washing services, especially when evaluating marketing and sales performance. CAC measures the cost incurred by the business to acquire a new customer, including marketing and advertising expenses. By comparing CAC to customer lifetime value (CLV), business owners can assess the effectiveness of their customer acquisition strategies and optimize marketing spend to acquire customers more cost-effectively.

Moreover, employee productivity and efficiency are critical KPIs for mobile car washing services. Labor costs typically represent a significant expense for mobile car washing businesses, making it essential to monitor employee productivity and efficiency. KPIs such as the number of cars serviced per hour per employee or labor cost per car wash can help business owners assess employee performance, identify training needs, and optimize staffing levels to maximize productivity and minimize costs.

Furthermore, environmental sustainability is an increasingly important KPI for mobile car washing services, reflecting growing consumer and regulatory concerns about environmental impact. KPIs such as water usage per car wash, energy consumption, and waste generation can help business owners assess their environmental footprint and identify opportunities for improvement. Implementing eco-friendly practices and technologies can not only reduce costs but also enhance the business's reputation and appeal to environmentally conscious customers.

In conclusion, Key Performance Indicators (KPIs) play a vital role in measuring and evaluating the performance of mobile car washing services. By monitoring KPIs related to customer satisfaction, service throughput, average revenue per car wash, customer acquisition cost, employee productivity, and environmental sustainability, business owners can gain valuable insights into their operations, identify areas for improvement, and drive growth and profitability in the competitive mobile car washing industry.

Making Informed Decisions

In the realm of mobile car washing services, making informed decisions is the cornerstone of success. Whether it's determining pricing strategies, expanding service offerings, or investing in new equipment, every decision can significantly impact the business's performance and profitability. By leveraging data, market insights, and industry knowledge, mobile car washing service owners can make informed decisions that drive growth, enhance customer satisfaction, and ensure long-term success in the competitive marketplace.

One crucial aspect of making informed decisions in the mobile car washing industry is understanding customer preferences and market trends. By analyzing customer feedback, reviews, and market research data, business owners can gain valuable insights into consumer preferences, behaviors, and expectations. For example, understanding which car washing services are in high demand or which areas have a concentration of potential customers can help business owners tailor their offerings and marketing strategies to meet market demand effectively.

Moreover, data-driven decision-making is essential for optimizing operational efficiency and resource allocation in mobile car washing services. By analyzing key performance indicators (KPIs) such as service throughput, labor productivity, and equipment utilization, business owners can identify inefficiencies, streamline workflows, and allocate resources more effectively. For instance, analyzing service throughput data can help business owners optimize scheduling and routing to minimize downtime and maximize revenue-generating opportunities.

Financial analysis and planning are also critical components of making informed decisions in the mobile car washing industry. By regularly reviewing financial statements, tracking expenses, and monitoring cash flow, business owners can assess their financial health and identify areas for cost reduction or revenue growth. Financial forecasting and budgeting can help business owners anticipate future expenses, plan for investments, and ensure financial stability and sustainability.

Furthermore, staying abreast of industry regulations and compliance requirements is essential for making informed decisions in the mobile car washing industry. Compliance with local regulations, environmental standards, and health and safety protocols is not only essential for avoiding penalties and legal issues but also for maintaining the business's reputation and integrity. By staying informed about regulatory changes and industry best practices, business owners can ensure compliance and mitigate risks effectively.

In addition to data and market insights, intuition and experience also play a role in making informed decisions in the mobile car washing industry. While data and analytics provide valuable insights, business owners must also trust their instincts and draw upon their industry knowledge and expertise when making decisions. Combining data-driven insights with intuition and experience can help business owners make well-rounded and informed decisions that align with their business goals and values.

Moreover, collaboration and consultation with stakeholders, employees, and industry experts can enrich the decision-making process in mobile car washing services. Seeking input and feedback from team members, customers, and business partners can provide valuable perspectives and insights that may not have been considered otherwise. Additionally, networking with industry peers and participating in professional associations can facilitate knowledge sharing and collaboration, enabling business owners to make more informed decisions.

In conclusion, making informed decisions is essential for success in the mobile car washing industry. By leveraging data, market insights, financial analysis, industry knowledge, intuition, and collaboration, business owners can make decisions that drive growth, enhance operational efficiency, and ensure compliance with regulations. In the fast-paced and competitive mobile car washing market, informed decision-making is the key to staying ahead of the curve and achieving long-term success.

Growing and Expanding Your Business

Growing and Expanding Your Mobile Car Washing Business

In the dynamic and competitive world of mobile car washing services, expanding and growing your business is essential for staying ahead of the competition and maximizing profitability. Whether you're looking to increase your customer base, expand your service offerings, or enter new markets, strategic growth and expansion initiatives can drive success and long-term sustainability for your mobile car washing business.

One key strategy for growing your mobile car washing business is to focus on customer acquisition and retention. By implementing targeted marketing campaigns, leveraging digital marketing channels, and offering promotions and discounts, you can attract new customers and expand your customer base. Additionally, prioritizing customer satisfaction, providing exceptional service, and fostering loyalty programs can help retain existing customers and generate repeat business, driving sustainable growth over time.

Moreover, expanding your service offerings can be a lucrative strategy for growing your mobile car washing business. In addition to traditional car washing services, consider diversifying your offerings to include detailing services, interior cleaning, waxing, and other value-added services. By meeting the diverse needs and preferences of your customers, you can increase revenue streams, attract a broader customer base, and differentiate your business from competitors in the market.

Furthermore, expanding your geographic reach and entering new markets can unlock new growth opportunities for your mobile car washing business. Consider expanding into adjacent neighborhoods, commercial areas, or new cities to reach untapped customer segments and increase market share. Conduct market research to identify high-demand areas and assess competition, demographics, and customer preferences to inform your expansion strategy effectively.

In addition to geographic expansion, strategic partnerships and collaborations can also facilitate business growth and expansion in the mobile car washing industry. Consider partnering with local businesses, such as auto dealerships, car rental agencies, or property management companies, to offer exclusive discounts or bundled services to their customers. Collaborating with complementary businesses can help you access new customer segments, expand your brand reach, and drive mutual growth and success.

Moreover, investing in technology and innovation can fuel growth and expansion for your mobile car washing business. Consider adopting mobile apps for scheduling and booking appointments, implementing automated payment systems, or incorporating eco-friendly cleaning solutions and equipment. Embracing technology and innovation can enhance operational efficiency, improve customer experience, and position your business for future growth and scalability.

Additionally, scaling your operations and optimizing resource allocation are essential considerations when growing and expanding your mobile car washing business. Evaluate your current business processes, workflows, and staffing levels to identify inefficiencies and opportunities for improvement. Invest in training and development for your team members, streamline operations, and leverage technology solutions to increase productivity and scalability as you expand your business.

Furthermore, maintaining a strong brand identity and reputation is crucial for sustained growth and expansion in the mobile car washing industry. Focus on delivering consistent quality service, exceeding customer expectations, and actively soliciting feedback to continuously improve and evolve your business. Invest in branding initiatives, online reputation management, and customer engagement strategies to build brand loyalty and trust, driving customer retention and advocacy.

In conclusion, growing and expanding your mobile car washing business requires careful planning, strategic decision-making, and a commitment to delivering exceptional service. By focusing on customer acquisition and retention, expanding service offerings, entering new markets, forming strategic partnerships, embracing technology and innovation, optimizing operations, and building a strong brand reputation, you can drive sustainable growth and success for your mobile car washing business in the competitive marketplace.

Developing Business Growth Strategies

In the realm of mobile car washing services, developing effective business growth strategies is paramount to staying competitive and achieving long-term success. With the right strategies in place, mobile car washing businesses can expand their customer base, increase revenue, and solidify their position in the market. Here are some key strategies to consider when developing growth plans for your mobile car washing service:

First and foremost, one of the fundamental strategies for business growth is to focus on customer acquisition and retention. Mobile car washing businesses can attract new customers by offering promotions, discounts, and referral programs, as well as leveraging digital marketing channels such as social media, search engine optimization (SEO), and online advertising. Additionally, providing exceptional service, exceeding customer expectations, and fostering loyalty programs can help retain existing customers and generate repeat business, driving sustainable growth over time.

Expanding service offerings is another effective strategy for business growth in the mobile car washing industry. In addition to traditional car washing services, consider diversifying your offerings to include detailing services, interior cleaning, waxing, and other value-added services. By meeting the diverse needs and preferences of your customers, you can increase revenue streams, attract a broader customer base, and differentiate your business from competitors in the market.

Moreover, geographic expansion can unlock new growth opportunities for mobile car washing businesses. Consider expanding into adjacent neighborhoods, commercial areas, or new cities to reach untapped customer segments and increase market share. Conducting thorough market research to identify high-demand areas and assess competition, demographics, and customer preferences can inform your expansion strategy effectively and help you capitalize on growth opportunities.

Strategic partnerships and collaborations can also facilitate business growth and expansion in the mobile car washing industry. Consider partnering with local businesses such as auto dealerships, car rental agencies, or property management companies to offer exclusive discounts or bundled services to their customers. Collaborating with complementary businesses can help you access new customer segments, expand your brand reach, and drive mutual growth and success.

Investing in technology and innovation is another key strategy for business growth in the mobile car washing industry. Adopting mobile apps for scheduling and booking appointments, implementing automated payment systems, or incorporating eco-friendly cleaning solutions and equipment can enhance operational efficiency, improve customer experience, and position your business for future growth and scalability.

Furthermore, scaling operations and optimizing resource allocation are essential considerations when developing business growth strategies for mobile car washing services. Evaluate current business processes, workflows, and staffing levels to identify inefficiencies and opportunities for improvement. Investing in training and development for team members, streamlining operations, and leveraging technology solutions can increase productivity and scalability as you expand your business.

Maintaining a strong brand identity and reputation is crucial for sustained growth and expansion in the mobile car washing industry. Focus on delivering consistent quality service, exceeding customer expectations, and actively soliciting feedback to continuously improve and evolve your business. Invest in branding initiatives, online reputation management, and customer engagement strategies to build brand loyalty and trust, driving customer retention and advocacy.

In conclusion, developing effective business growth strategies is essential for mobile car washing businesses to thrive and succeed in a competitive marketplace. By focusing on customer acquisition and retention, expanding service offerings, geographic expansion, strategic partnerships, technology and innovation, scaling operations, and building a strong brand reputation, mobile car washing services can drive sustainable growth and achieve long-term success.

Franchising Your Business

Franchising Your Mobile Car Washing Business: A Path to Expansion and Success

Franchising has become a popular growth strategy for businesses across various industries, offering entrepreneurs the opportunity to expand their brand presence, increase market share, and generate additional revenue streams. For mobile car washing businesses looking to scale operations and reach new markets, franchising can be an attractive option. Let's explore the benefits, considerations, and steps involved in franchising your mobile car washing business.

One of the primary advantages of franchising your mobile car washing business is accelerated growth and market expansion. By granting franchise opportunities to aspiring entrepreneurs, you can rapidly expand your brand presence into new territories, cities, or regions without the need for significant upfront capital investment or operational resources. Franchisees bring local market knowledge, customer relationships, and entrepreneurial drive, enabling your business to penetrate new markets more effectively.

Franchising also allows you to leverage the passion and commitment of franchisees to drive business success. As independent business owners, franchisees are highly motivated to grow their individual franchises and uphold the brand's reputation and standards. This decentralized business model empowers franchisees to make operational decisions tailored to their local market needs while adhering to the overarching brand guidelines and standards set by the franchisor.

Moreover, franchising your mobile car washing business can generate additional revenue streams through franchise fees, ongoing royalties, and other revenue-sharing arrangements. Franchise fees typically cover the initial franchise setup, training, and support provided to new franchisees, while ongoing royalties are calculated as a percentage of the franchisee's sales or profits. These revenue streams can contribute to the financial sustainability and profitability of your business over the long term.

However, franchising your mobile car washing business requires careful planning, preparation, and execution to ensure success. Before embarking on the franchising journey, it's essential to assess your business's readiness and suitability for franchising. Evaluate factors such as the strength of your brand, the scalability of your business model, and the availability of operational systems and processes that can be replicated across multiple locations.

Developing a comprehensive franchise program is a critical step in franchising your mobile car washing business. This program should include detailed franchise agreements, operating manuals, training programs, marketing support, and ongoing operational assistance to help franchisees launch and operate their businesses successfully. Working with legal and franchise consultants can ensure that your franchise program complies with regulatory requirements and best practices in the franchising industry.

Selecting the right franchisees is another crucial aspect of franchising your mobile car washing business. Look for individuals who share your passion for the industry, possess strong business acumen, and are committed to upholding your brand's values and standards. Conduct thorough due diligence, interviews, and background checks to ensure that prospective franchisees have the necessary skills, experience, and financial resources to succeed.

Providing comprehensive training and ongoing support to franchisees is essential for their success and the overall success of your franchised network. Offer training programs covering all aspects of operating a mobile car washing business, including technical skills, customer service, sales and marketing, and business management. Additionally, establish channels for ongoing communication, mentorship, and collaboration to foster a strong franchisee-franchisor relationship.

In conclusion, franchising your mobile car washing business can be a viable strategy for achieving growth, expansion, and success in the competitive marketplace. By leveraging the passion and resources of franchisees, generating additional revenue streams, and extending your brand presence into new markets, franchising offers numerous benefits for mobile car washing businesses. However, it's essential to approach franchising with careful planning, preparation, and commitment to ensure that both franchisors and franchisees thrive in the franchised network.

Exit Strategy and Selling Your Business

Exiting Your Mobile Car Washing Business: Strategies for a Successful Sale

While building and growing a mobile car washing business can be a rewarding endeavor, there may come a time when you decide to pursue other opportunities or retire from entrepreneurship. Planning for an exit strategy and selling your business can ensure a smooth transition while maximizing the value of your investment. Let's explore some key considerations and strategies for selling your mobile car washing business.

Firstly, it's essential to conduct a thorough assessment of your business's financial health, operations, and market position before putting it up for sale. This includes compiling financial statements, profit and loss statements, and other relevant documentation to provide prospective buyers with a clear understanding of your business's performance and potential. Additionally, evaluate your customer base, market share, and competitive landscape to identify selling points and areas for improvement.

Determining the appropriate valuation for your mobile car washing business is another critical step in the selling process. Consider factors such as revenue, profitability, growth potential, assets, and market trends when valuing your business. Seeking assistance from business valuation experts or professional advisors can help ensure that your business is priced competitively and attractively to potential buyers.

Preparing your business for sale involves addressing any operational or financial issues, streamlining processes, and enhancing its overall appeal to potential buyers. This may include investing in equipment upgrades, improving customer relationships, and implementing marketing initiatives to increase brand awareness and market visibility. Presenting a well-maintained and profitable business can significantly enhance its attractiveness to prospective buyers.

When it comes to marketing your mobile car washing business for sale, utilizing various channels and networks can help reach a broader audience of potential buyers. Consider listing your business on online marketplaces, business brokerage websites, and industry-specific platforms to attract qualified buyers. Additionally, leverage your professional network, industry associations, and referrals to identify potential buyers who may be interested in acquiring your business.

Engaging the services of a reputable business broker or intermediary can also facilitate the selling process and ensure a successful transaction. Business brokers have expertise in marketing businesses for sale, negotiating with buyers, and navigating the complexities of the sales process. They can help you identify qualified buyers, negotiate favorable terms, and facilitate a smooth transition of ownership.

Negotiating the terms of the sale is a critical aspect of selling your mobile car washing business. Consider factors such as the sale price, payment terms, transition period, and any contingencies or conditions of the sale. Be prepared to negotiate with potential buyers to reach a mutually beneficial agreement that meets your financial objectives and ensures a successful transition of ownership.

Once you've reached an agreement with a buyer, it's essential to finalize the sale through a legally binding contract and ensure all necessary legal and regulatory requirements are met. This may include obtaining licenses and permits, transferring leases or contracts, and addressing any outstanding liabilities or obligations. Working with legal advisors or attorneys can help ensure that the sale process is completed smoothly and in compliance with relevant laws and regulations.

In conclusion, planning for an exit strategy and selling your mobile car washing business requires careful preparation, strategic marketing, and effective negotiation skills. By assessing your business's value, preparing it for sale, marketing it to potential buyers, and negotiating favorable terms, you can achieve a successful sale and transition of ownership. Whether you're looking to pursue new opportunities or retire from entrepreneurship, selling your mobile car washing business can be a rewarding and lucrative endeavor with the right approach and preparation

Have Questions / Comments?

This book was designed to cover as much as possible but I know I have probably missed something, or some new amazing discovery that has just come out.

If you notice something missing or have a question that I failed to answer, please get in touch and let me know. If I can, I will email you an answer and also update the book so others can also benefit from it.

Thanks For Being Awesome :)

Submit Your Questions / Comments At:

https://xspurts.com/posts/questions

Get Another Book Free

We love writing and have produced a huge number of books.

For being one of our amazing readers, we would love to offer you another book we have created, 100% free.

To claim this limited time special offer, simply go to the site below and enter your name and email address.

You will then receive one of my great books, direct to your email account, 100% free!

https://xspurts.com/posts/free-book-offer

www.ingramcontent.com/pod-product-compliance
Lightning Source LLC
Chambersburg PA
CBHW071048290526
45795CB00004B/1392